I0465893

Never Go Broke Again With Fast Credit Repair

By: Emmanuel Loncke

LEGAL NOTICE

THE PUBLISHER HAS APPEARED TO BE
COMPLETE AND AS PRECISE AS POSSIBLE IN
THE DEVELOPMENT OF THE REPORT HE
DOESN'T WARRANT OR REPRESENT THAT THE
CONTENTS ARE BECAUSE OF THE CHANGING
NATURE OF THE NET.

SUCH AS ANYTHING IN LIFE, IN ADVICE
PUBLICATIONS, THERE ARE NO WARRANTIES OF
EARNINGS. CLIENTS ARE CAUTIONED TO
ANSWER IN THEIR OWN JUDGMENT
REGARDING THEIR SITUATION TO BEHAVE.

THIS PUBLICATION ISN'T MEANT AS A SOURCE
OF ACCOUNTING, BUSINESS, LEGAL OR
FINANCIAL INFORMATION. ALL SUBSCRIBERS
ARE ADVISED TO SEEK PROFESSIONAL
SERVICES OF PROFESSIONALS.

THIS MANUAL IS WRITTEN IN ARIAL YOU ARE
INVITED TO PUBLISH THIS PUBLICATION FOR
READING.

TABLE OF CONTENTS

For information on personal credit dispute letters go to www.nbacreditrepair.com

INTRODUCTION

Credit Repair is described as a way of disputing or rectifying discrepancies exhibited on credit bureau reports to be able to acquire the best and most precise evaluations for customers.

One of the most essential things to consider back is seeing credit issues and this means you are not the only person who's suffering from bad credit.

On the opposing side, you will find countless honorable, hard-working individuals from all over the country that are currently experiencing or have endured problems with their credit also.

Nonetheless, your consciousness of the significance of getting great credit has set you one step nearer to really achieving a fantastic credit score and enhancing your quality of living. Despite the fact that your credit score may look like an intangible asset, it's among the very valuable and significant assets you have.

To be able to acquire the privilege of working with a credit card, your credit score is assessed. If a business decides your charge to be disappointing, you'll be denied.

If you cannot get a credit card, then you cannot lease a car, arrange tickets, or perhaps rent a movie. Since your credit score has been determined to be disappointing, most firms won't allow you to use their cash.

Nowadays more than ever, many companies perform regular background checks through the hiring process. Yet more, in case your credit score shows something of concern with these, you'll be turned off for employment.

Since keeping a fantastic credit score is important in the modern society, a bad credit score could have a negative effect toward your own personal objectives. Great, string credit lets you reside with financial protection and allows you to buy things without depleting your lifetime savings.

Fixing your credit can look like a monumental undertaking nonetheless, it may also be as simple as wiring a letter or making a telephone call. The longer you spend now toward strengthening your credit score, the greater the quality of life is.

This manual is meant to support and assist families and individuals find the answers to the most frequently asked questions of credit fix, in addition to telling them of the risks that lurk the market.

CHAPTER 1 - BUILD YOUR SURVIVAL FOUNDATION

Why is it important to have a good credit?

With today's society becoming more and more business oriented, establishing and maintaining good credit is vital if you plan to do any of the following:

1. Apply for employment
2. Rent an apartment
3. Open a bank account
4. Setup an account with public service or the telephone company

It was that establishing excellent credit was significant only if you planned to purchase a house or automobile, but not anymore. The easiest task, like applying for employment might very much signify that you will need a fantastic credit.

Having poor credit may impede your ability to endure. That is sad to state but it's an established truth that people are turned down high excellent job positions just due to their credit score in spite of the fact that particular job might be precisely what a individual has to repair their credit score. That is a frightening grab twenty-two do not you believe?

Ok, I am caught in that terrifying grab twenty-two, what if I do?

You're entitled by Federal Law to be given a free yearly credit report. There are 3 primary credit-reporting agencies which you have to contact, you are able to conduct a search online or even locate their data in a telephone book. In Case You Have already obtained a credit report for that year, then you may also utilize any letter of credit refusal by sending in a copy of that letter within 60 days of its receipt with your written request. Make sure you include a copy of your state issued ID, your last known addresses for the previous five decades along with proof of your address.

It is important to add a copy of your social security card. What does it mean to have good credit? Who cares who sees it? Your credit report is advice to anyone where you're requesting a credit line.

Whenever you make an application for a flat, employment, or try to create a purchase, you are currently requesting credit and allowing the lender to observe your credit report. Though your credit report doesn't show a character diagnose, it might just as well, considering it's via your credit report the way others (prospective creditors) will comprehend what sort of person you're.

Firms decide from your capacity to pay and look into your own credit report and follow through what type of person you're.

Can you stick to your own promises?

Would you follow through online obligations are you currently really stable?

In that case, then you are an individual that is good and trustworthy.

You could possibly be well worth living in that community, or giving an opportunity at that job that is ideal.

What about people with poor credit?

You Might Be a person that is Fantastic, you may be the most considerate and compassionate person alive if your credit report shows a payment

or no payment on an account at all, Your being may be perceived rather than dependable, unstable and untrustworthy. Prepare to take care of a great deal of telephone and paperwork time as soon as you're prepared to fix your credit score.

This signifies is that it's time for you. Your earnings could be restricted or null, that is ok, there is a means to save your standing that is own personal and open doors of opportunity. When you get your credit report(s), contact the lenders recorded and make payment arrangements, even if it's only $1-$5 per month. Doing so reveals your willingness it show that you're currently putting effort towards establishing obligation and stability.

Whom can I turn to for assistance? What does this mean? How do I protect my reputation?

There are a number of tools available to help with credit repair, use the web or your library. Credit repair bureaus provide services that are free, make the most of help and the offers. Building your credit is having the ability to generate a buy, in addition, it means you establishing your success base and are setting your reputation that is own personal.

ESSENTIALS TO REPAIRING YOUR CREDIT

There are essentials to repairing your credit and building your history. It depends on your situation, but in most cases you can find a way out of any debt situation. Debt relief is a stressful situation. When times are hard the last thing we need is to add more stress to our lives. Therefore we want to start out by acknowledging the problems in front of us. Once we acknowledge the problem we can take the next step to find a resolve.

Now that we have some essential steps to repairing credit, we next want to review some of the options available to us. There are many steps we can take to eliminating debt. Repairing your credit means that you must learn the different scams on the marketplace to avoid complicating your situation and adding to your debts.

Telemarketers that claim to get you out of debt in three minutes are obviously scammers that are trying to make a buck. Anyone that tells you they can help you get out of debt and charge you are fee are basically a source of scammers.

The best solution then for getting out of debt is learning to rely on yourself. Repairing credit has its good and bad essentials. The basic rule of thumb is to search a way that works best for your situation. Today we are going to take a look at some of the good basics in credit repair.

If you are in debt and own a home you probably have insurance coverage. If so you might be able to take an advance payment against your insurance. Life Insurance Coverage may offer a payback solution after you have paid in on the plan for a length of time.

It might be wise to check out your policy to see if there is some type of disbursement plan available. If you are able to get a lump sum be sure to pay off your debts rather than spending your money freely. You may even want to check into your Home Mortgage agreement and the insurance coverage available.

If you are suffering debt problems related to injuries or even suffer a Terminal Illness some policies will make payments on your mortgage until you are back on your feet again. If you are off work due to unemployed as no result of your own then you may be qualified on your insurance policy a coverage that makes your payments until you are back at work.

3

If you don't have insurance coverage you might or you have insurance coverage that doesn't offer this options you may want to check with your lender to find out if there is a refinance loan available to you that offers lower monthly installments and lower interest rates.

If you get into another loan you want to make sure that you are not paying more than you already are. If you decide to take out a refinance loan make sure that you are aware of the upfront fees that often are included in mortgage loans.

What about car payments?

Are you paying a fortune on your car each month?

If so there maybe an option that can get you some relief. You may be able to refinance your car, or else sell your car, making more money than what you owe on your loan. The extra cash can be spent toward a good used car. Sometimes used cars tend to last longer than newer cars and are less expensive to maintenance. Also, you could look into a repossession of the vehicle if your situation is out of hand. This will go against your credit report, but when there is no other solution sometimes we have to toss in the towel.

Finally, you can increase your income by selling valuable assets or else finding a job that pays more for your worth. Sometimes we work and are paid less than what we deserve, so if there is a solution available by all means jump on it.

Repairing credit has many essentials, but for the most part credit repair is just an illusion where many people do not take the step to repair.

STEPS TO CREDIT REPAIR

When the creditors or agencies file a false claim in your own credit report you may be qualified to sue the computers. Whether there are claims against you in your report the very first step would be to submit a dispute against the promises. This will delay your obligations and if you do not owe the bill it may spare you from the debt when the agencies discover that you aren't responsible. The changes in legislation are making it hard for customers to restore their credit, however some guidelines into regulations make it feasible to receive all three of your credit reports at no cost.

In case you've got a credit record of neglect you want to have copies of your credit reports to be certain no false allegations were made against you personally. Experian, TransUnion, and Equifax have a dare hotline available. Disputing is a step in the ideal way for fixing your credit score. Nearly all information in your credit reports is out of banks, credit card companies, utilities suppliers, decisions, and so forth.

It's necessary that you contact the agencies as soon as possible if you see any claims made against you which you believe aren't your responsibility. Credit repair isn't always easy, however there are alternatives available to help us get out of debt. Most of us have bills and occasionally these bills are crazy. Paying bills is continuing, there's absolutely not any escape so the best potential alternative then is requesting assistance and working to settle your debts.

Your information normally remains on your credit report for 7 decades.

Favorable results frequently remain on your accounts for about ten decades. Tax exemptions often remain on your credit history for about 15 decades and bankruptcies often remain on your credit report for a decade.

It's prudent to submit a dispute In case you have any debts in your credit report which don't belong to you. The agencies will look into the accusations and then they're going to get rid of the asserts, if they discover it's incorrect. The businesses delete or alter the claims from you if the information in your credit report doesn't have any resolve. That is the reason why it's very important to keep tabs on your credit report. You receive details and may see your credit rating.

If you can not appear to discover a solution and understand there are, it's best to get educated. Then you're misled if you think credit repair companies which claim that they can remove items and reduce your monthly debts. The law regulates The majority of the businesses.

In other words, the government has reason to think that their customers may be misled by the businesses. The majority of the companies which claim they can get you out of debt in no time or little are waiting to take cash from out of the pocket. Should you require support or assistance with your own credit it's sensible to go.

The agents are trained in helping customers find a remedy. They will help get the creditors off your back. It's very important that you learn your rights if you're looking for a way to fix your credit score and in debt. Is difficult generally, but not hopeless.

Millions around the planet at the same time or the other has some change which has affected them. You are not alone and you will find many which are mindful of this actuality.

The Consumer Response Center is a great source for finding information about your rights. In some cases, some of us have more rights than others.

Victims of Identity Theft or Military Personnel that have been robbed of their identity have more rights than people delinquent of paying on time. Knowing what is available to you is the first step to repairing your credit and getting back on track.

REPAIRING YOUR CREDIT RATINGS

Is your wish?

Then before starting in building your credit score, you may wish to think about several factors. Credit is bad in a few ways, and great in a variety of ways. Credit puts pressure on us because to be able to have the respect we 21, we must keep a score.

Most of us have a few us do and our struggles in life. There are lots of reasons a individual's credit is faulty. We need to keep a high level of precision or else. Since we don't enjoy for else' we need to find a remedy to maintain our credit score. The qualities about credit would be that it provides a settlement to you when times are tough, and if you would like to construct credit.

To begin fixing your own credit you have to hunt. Is get copies of your credit reports. The drawback is if you don't apply for a credit card or loan, that need to be responsible for the reports. Make sure you avoid using for loans and cards because the longer you employ the more your own credit ratings affect.

As soon as you submit an application for credit or a loan, the creditors will ask for copies of your credit file, which adds a credit rating and points and it remains on your account for about 3 decades. The more things you have, it takes. Then you've got one benefit of obtaining all accounts free As soon as you apply for a credit card loan.

Today everybody is assessing account, which means that your score is influenced in 1 way or another. Now every company will assess your credit file, so if you're currently purchasing a car avert allowing the sales reps until you understand this is exactly what you desire to look at your credit.

It's helpful to bring an updated credit report, which many creditors will tell you we cannot use this." That is ok; inform the repetitions" that you aren't assessing my charge until I understand that is what I need to do." The credit report may supply a summary of what they're taking a look at to them.

UNDERSTANDING THE FACT

As soon as your credit reports have been asked by you, you can move on the next step. Report that seems questionable make certain to contact the 3 credit bureaus petitioning the charges In case you have any charges on your credit.

The claims from the report affect you personally, so you've got the right to submit a claim with the Fair Crediting Reporting Act (FCRA). Back in 1971, the US Congress passed a law to shield us against claims registered.

Make the most of this legislation. Knowing the steps is vital to have on the path. You may need to wait prior to applying for a loan or credit card As soon as you have disputed your credit reports mistakes. After about half a year, many credit agencies eliminate the mistakes.

Because in some instances they fail to eliminate the errors be aware that you might need to contend with the agencies. Any delinquencies on your credit report be In case you have, certain if at all possible, to look after them immediately. The six weeks be confident you keep on paying your debts As you wait. If you don't have enough money make certain that you make payments that are decent on the invoice to prevent credit reports.

Ensure you satisfy all payments if you would like to submit an application for a loan afterwards. Additionally, it's best to maintain an updated copy of your own credit report available when at all possible. We're advised to track our credit reports. Taking the initial step is the start of building a fantastic credit rating and score, if your purpose is to fix your own credit.

UNDERSTANDING CREDIT FILES

If you're credit history using a minimal score landlords, lenders, or suppliers will probably turn you down when you apply for financing. Credit files are usually found in the computer systems are kept by credit reporting agencies. In case your credit file suggests you're a minimal risk then you probably will find financing, flat, credit card, or anything you employ for.

That is the reason why it's very important to establish credit at a young age. Should you apply for department store cards, charge cards, gasoline cards or other items offering you a charge, then you're in your way to establishing a credit history and your document is going to be on listing. The issue with applying for credit cards or cards, or any kind of charge, is when we begin our parents ' are often co-signers. This means that if we don't make payments our parents are bound to settle the debts. Credit ratings are a numerical' system which determines a individual's credit score and rate. Credit scores usually rate everywhere from '300 to 850' differently the scores are greater if a individual has an outstanding credit rate. If you submit an application for financing and the creditors are not able to locate your credit file you're often regarded as a mishap. This usually means you haven't established a credit history and nobody can tell if you're in good or poor risk.

If you're in debt and nagged every day by lenders you may want to comprehend your credit documents to fix your credit score. If you're delinquent in payments that your credit rating changed, and often you can not secure financing. There are exceptions however if you can have a loan or credit card you'll be paying high interest prices. Your credit file decides your beliefs in life.

The laws protect you from the feeling that it modulates the credit reporting agencies by simply letting them record negative reports from you for a limited time. The legislation also govern who can understand your credit documents. If you're asking for a loan, permit, public support, landlords, insurance, and courts may ask your credit documents without your approval.

But if you're asking for work under certain conditions the companies will require a written consent form from you. Utilities are within regulations and these suppliers can't deny you solutions even in the event that you've got terrible credit.

The reality is that if we apply for work, submit an application for a flat, or take out an insurance policy we're establishing credit. Your credit documents are usually stored in TransUnion, Equifax, and Experian. The legislation protects us to some level when it comes to credit repair. To know all of the legalities, in addition to the way our credit file changes us is essential to fixing our credit record.

This protects you if you're a victim of Identity Theft, or some other false accusations made against you personally. The credit reporting agencies are required by the legislation to record accuracies on credit documents by collecting the right information from you or in your behalf.

As you can see there are a vast assortment of services that could check your credit history. The drawback is every time your credit is assessed points go on your own files.

Credit Reporting Agencies are coordinated and monitored by the Federal Trade Commission under the Needs of this Federal Fair Credit Reporting Act (FCRA) and follows up with the State Laws. In case you have credit documents with inconsistencies that the Fair Credit Reporting Act protects you from the meaning that it takes the credit bureaus to delete or produce the information obsolete in your credit history.

In case you've got terrible credit and seeking to fix your credit then you definitely want to be certain to request copies of your credit documents, comprehend your score on your own documents, and if you suspect you're a risk it's ideal to apply for loans or credit cards as soon as you've eliminated your credit history. The further things added to your credit report changes your credit so that you would like to be cautious and just apply for whatever you want.

TAKES OBSERVATION

In case you've got invoices that are present and there are no late charges make certain to look after those bills by paying this is going to keep you from the credit 33, because. It's necessary that you get a fiscal situation to escape debt. If your job doesn't pay enough to make ends meet, you may want to discover work that pays salary that are . Do not wait till it's too late. If you're currently seeing a prognosis that is lousy but it is out of hands which you lost control, catch up and accept your hands back. You will find mortgages available offering underpayments and overpayments.

It may be smart to apply for a credit card which lets you pay off cards In case you have credit cards. There is a way to getting out of the debt. Again, the most significant instrument for getting out of debt is to keep watch payoff any bill as you move and work through every invoice.

Auto loans have been secured, and it's your duty. Some Department Store Credit Cards are procured, they also ask should you miss payments to the product you to put up security. Debts are so forth, and utilities, lease student loans, many credit cards. This implies that it's more important to repay bonded loans vs. unsecured loans. Loans are so forth, car payments and home payments. This could enable you to get out of debt. want to concentrate on your bills that are overdue As soon as you obtain your bills taking good care of you. Take good care of this invoice, In case you haven't attained the credit agency however. Working together with the legislation, I will tell you from hitting the credit agency that in the event that you make a tiny fee toward a bill it could save you. The truth is, if you're currently making any sort of attempt to pay off a invoice it might keep you.

Fixing your credit takes monitoring on your part. We get two kinds of invoices in the email. Are current. The simple fact is currently ignoring it doesn't help repair your credit score and your invoices is delaying. By dismissing loans that are secured which what you need to lose dismissing loans, You've got more to lose. In case you believe that you cannot make ends meet and have a Mortgage, you may want to check into a few of the alternatives. There could be a home loan or fantastic commodities which would enable you fix your credit score and to escape debt.

The majority of us have credit cards, credit cards, auto loans, house payments, and other kinds of loans . There are two sorts so to know these debts is essential to fixing your credit score. Loans are any debts which have security. Put simply your Mortgage is a loan that in the event that payment is missed by you may be living in the streets. Automobile loans are a method of getting back on your feet if you skip a few payments.

11

The most essential step to fixing credit is currently remaining current on your invoices if possible. It's sensible to make contact with the lender letting them know there'll be a delay 29, if you think you cannot make a payment. Creditors prefer that you call them to negotiate a payment strategy and creditors will decrease your invoice, or perhaps your monthly payments. The solution is currently celebrating, and making an attempt. This means the month, that you may overpay 1 month in your loan and underpay. A holiday pay is offered by A few of the loans. You are able to use the money if you do not need to go on holiday. These types of loans may be paid than other kinds of loans.

STOP, THINK AND LISTEN

One of the best tools for repairing credit is to stop, think, and listen. If you are in debt, you need to stop and think about your situation and stay alert to the activities on your credit report.

We are going to examine disadvantages and advantages available to you as the debtor. Let's take a look at what can happen when you have bad credit as well as what you can do to protect your self from the creditors and collection agencies. If you are obligated to pay child support, college tuitions, income tax, the IRS can take your money. This means each year that you miss payments are at default the IRS will deduct your entire tax refund to repay the debt.

The IRS is obligated to contact you before deducting any fees from your tax refunds. If you miss payments on Insurance Policies and you have conditions stipulated on that policy you may be at risk of loosing your property. If you have late bills on utilities, under law, (in most states) the utility providers cannot cut your heat during particular months stated in the law regardless of nonpayment's. Most states are required to give you a written notice before they can disconnect your service.

This will give you time to find the funds to pay toward your utilities. Likewise, some insurance policies will allow you a grace period toward your insurance. Anytime you are allowed time it is time to stop, think and listen. If you take the time to review your bills and funds and come to the conclusion you do not have enough to pay the entire amount of the bill, you might get away with minimal balance temporarily.

Paying something toward your bill is better than avoiding your obligations. Another point you want to keep in mind is that when creditors write off a debt you may be required to pay taxes on the bill. Once a creditor writes off a debt it is sent to the IRS for review and if they choose to do so, you will still pay on that bill at the end of the year.

So the best bet is when you get the first letter in the mail asking you to pay your bill is to write the lender or creditor and explain your situation politely and ask for an extension on payments. The truth is most creditors that lend or extend you credit hope that you are a returning customer and only suffering temporarily.

If you can keep the creditors on your side this is your best solution for avoiding complications. Another suggestion is to send in minimal payments on current bills that are overdue. Your next bill will be steep but if you keep sending minimal payments until you are caught up, your name will not go in a credit bureau. If creditors recommend that you send payment immediately to avoid hassles, disregard the creditor.

The creditor is doing nothing more but adding more expense to your debt. If you have a bill and have money to make payment tell the creditor that you will send the money through regular mail immediately. Do not waste money on services that will charge you to send a bill.

If you contact the creditors and they simply deny you the opportunity to extend your debt or ask for proof of your situation, it is time to make contact with a Debt Counselor. The Debt Counselor will work on your behalf to resolve the issue.

Do not argue or use foul language when you are addressing your debts, since this will only add more problems. If you have a bill, more than the time allowed for pay it is important that you DO NOT contact the creditors or collection agencies.

This is only letting the agencies know that you realize you owe the debt. By acknowledging, the debt will open up a new debt. Collection agencies and creditors pose a threat to millions of people each day, so the key to solving the problem is finding a solution to the problem. Stop, think and listen before you act.

USING PRE-PAID TO BUILDS CREDIT

If you are having difficulty with your credit score and rating, or having a hard time getting a credit card you might want to consider a pre-paid card. Nowadays it is virtually impossible to purchase anything without a credit card. Lenders today are offering Pre-Paid Visa and Master Cards, which work like credit cards.

The procedure works like put money into an account and then you are able to use the cards like a regular credit card. No one will know the difference. Prepaid credit cards can be purchased at many stores or online. The downside is you have to pay a small fee when you open an account.

You want to be careful with which card you choose since some are expensive. After the account is open, you have to pay a small fee every time you make another deposit on your account. The upside about prepaid cards is that it can help repair your credit.

Another advantage is, if your credit is bad then the prepaid may be the only the solution for repairing credit. The best solution is to continue paying your bills and avoid spending money on items you do not really need.

Most people spend a fortune during the course of a decade on various items all to sell them later in a garage sale, or else toss them in the garbage when they realize they did not need it in the first place. It pays to consider all aspects of any decision made to avoid complications. Bad credit is an obstacle and in order to defeat the obstacle you have to take steps to resolve the issues.

THE IMPORTANCE OF CREDIT REPORTS

Don't let bad credit ruin your life. We all have difficulties and sometimes we can't avoid obstacles that get in our way. It is important that you know your credit report status first before taking steps to repair your credit. Building credit is important, but if you do not know the basics, it is almost impossible to get out of debt.

Sure, you get bills in the mail everyday that tell you what you owe. You might even get annoying phone calls regularly to remind you of the mistakes made. Having your credit report on hand can save despair since some charges against individuals are mistakes. If you know what you owe, you are in the heading in the right direction to repairing your credit.

Credit reports can be obtained at any of the three credit bureaus including <u>Equifax</u>, <u>TransUnion</u>, and <u>Experian</u>. Some people will tell you to apply for a loan so that you can get a copy of your report free. This is ludicrous since each time you apply for a loan or credit card it goes against your score.

Why not pay $60 dollars now and save a fortune in the long run?

Most credit reports cost around $20 or more, but if you think about it, it will cost less later on. If you are building credit, you need to consider both long and short-term obstacles. There is nothing in life that is free, and that includes making the right decisions. Prepaid cards are a great start in the right direction for building your credit, but for the most part the cards offer nothing in line of restoring ultimate credit results.

The prepaid cards are treated like credit cards in one way, but it slowly builds or restores credit, so the process of credit repairing is only delayed yet obtainable. There are other types of credit cards available that claim to help restore your credit rating and score. Some of the card providers offer a lump sum of credit, but you have to pay around $200 or $300 upfront. The disadvantage is that some of these companies are fraudulent and work hard at taking your money, at the same time providing you no results.

Consumers such as Trust Benefit have taking money from consumers promising them a repair solution on their credit report. Once the company takes the money, they may or may not send you a credit card. Be careful! It pays to check with the <u>Better Business Bureau</u> (BBB) before you apply for a credit card to make sure the provider is not out to take you for a ride..

CHAPTER 2 – ASSUMPTIONS & PREVENTIONS

When it comes to life the majority are always assuming, and the most of them assume the worst. Creditors, debtors or anyone today all base their theories on assumptions and assumptions from the beginning of time have caused nothing but failure.

When people fail to pay their bills on time, many of the creditors assume that the debtor does not have the means to pay the debt. Many creditors with the assumption that you are not capable of paying your bills will often set up an arrangement or else lower the amount so that you can repay the debt.

This is a step to credit repair, however it takes you to contact the creditors to let them know your situation. If you have several bills on hand and all the bills are pressing it makes sense to pay off the debt that benefits you the most. After this bill is paid you can set aside an amount the following paycheck to pay off another of the bills. Once you follow this strategy it allows you to work your bills down gradually thus repairing your credit.

If you don't have the funds to repay the entire bill at most pay the minimum amount so that you can continue using the service. Most debtors assume they are in debt and there is nothing they can do to resolve the problems that plague their lives every day. Creditors are always on their back, and their paychecks are never enough to make ends meet. This is the process of giving up on life. When we give up it often leads to stress. The answer is often in front of them or comes somewhere down the line.

Sometimes we see Credit Counseling or Debt Consolidation advertisings, we will think, *"how can they help me"*. The fact is Debt Consolidation is only a lead to get creditors off your back for a moment. Credit Counselors are more prone to help you find a solution to repairing your credit. Credit Counselors is the solution when you don't see a way out on your own. The professionals work closely with your creditors, you, and work toward a resolve.

This is certainly a way to get creditors off your back, work out an agreement with your debts, and reduce the stress level that comes along with financial burdens. Some of the Credit Counseling Services offer a low fee for their services and provide you with a financial managing solution. The services often offer help with managing your money, as well as offering counseling to homeowners, students, and so on.

There are many solutions for debt relief so the key then is not assuming the worst. Again the main solution is paying off the debts that are considered priorities. If you have secured loans it is always wise to find a way to pay these bills first. Unsecured loans pose a threat, but nothing compared to secured debts. Some of the nonessential bills can include credit cards.

Although you are responsible for this bill, however the worst case that happens with credit cards is that you loose out all your privileges. Check your terms & agreements, since some credit cards may allow you to pay the interest on the cards. This will give you the time you need to find a solution for paying off the card. Some cards may even allow you to pay the minimum balance on the card and allow you to keep the card in your possession.

If you have credit cards you might want to consider paying your bills, which will give you time to repay the credit card. Pay the maximum amount on the credit card before the bill comes in so that you have funds available to pay your bills the following month in case you don't have the funds available. There is always a solution, so never assume that you can't deal with any problem.

You might want to cut back on some of your spending so that you will have extra cash when those bills come in also. Cutting back only provides a solution for gaining money and repairing your credit.

AVOIDING BAD CREDIT AND REPAIR CREDIT

HASSLES

Staying in contact with your payments each month can help you avoid bad credit. If you research the marketplace before coming to a purchasing decision, you are well on your way to avoiding bad credit and repair credit hassles. You want to consider all applications, including credit cards, student loans, mortgages, and car loans carefully to avoid being overcharged.

Making the wise decision ahead of the game is the ultimate solution to maintaining good credit. Most people when taking out a home mortgage loan are not aware of the options available to them. Many will walk in the bank door, fill out the application, and accept the terms & conditions when offered to them.

If you ever heard the many reports that swept the pages of newspapers, television and other advertising sources...families and individuals are filing bankruptcy because they cannot afford their homes anymore. This is because these people did not take the time to check the marketplace first and searching the options available to them. As you can see, the millions reported are in debt and searching for a way to repair their credit.

The solution then to avoiding bad credit and repair is to research, invest wisely, make good decisions, and budget. Being informed and educated is two of the best tools offered to us. There are mortgage loans that offer overpayments and underpayments and these loans include vacation packages and lump sum payments to the borrowers.

There are also other loans available that offer low mortgage monthly installments and low interest rates with insurance policies attached that will pay your mortgage if you are sick, unemployed, in an accident and so on.

On the other hand, there are mortgage loans that have high interest rates, high mortgages, and balloon payments attached. When balloon payments are attached to home mortgages it is almost guaranteed in a few years you will be searching for a solution to repair your credit. There are very few home lenders willing to tell you the truth about the variety of home loans available. Most of the lenders are making money and you are a source of income.

It is important to scope the terms & agreements carefully as well as reading all fine prints on any loan contract before you sign. If you want to avoid bad credit and repair, you want to stay on the right path. Loans are agreements that are made between two parties and attached are interest rates and other fees.

If you are applying for a home loan and want to avoid bad credit, it makes sense to learn what are the fees included and how much they are. Anytime you take out a mortgage loan there are upfront fees attached. In some cases, you can get a home for little or no cost. Searching the marketplace can save you time and money.

Some home loans offer an **'acceleration clause'**, which covers you if you miss mortgage payments. The lender will apply the clause by allowing you leniency providing you make payments the following month on time. This type of loan is great for avoiding bad credit, foreclosures, and repossessions. The marketplace is swarming with realtors and other sources that will help you get a mortgage loan affordable to you with benefits included.

Car Loans:

If you are applying for a car loan, it is also important to research the marketplace carefully before agreeing to any terms & conditions. Make sure that your find the best deals affordable to you.

College Loans:

College I learned a golden rule that applies to everyone. This rule is that most car dealers up the fees on cars 15%. This means if you negotiate with the dealer you can get a reduction on the vehicle up to 15%.

Credit Cards:

Another word of advice is when applying for credit cards you want to sway away from cards that have fees attached and high interest rates. Avoid credit card offers that have upfront fees offer a high line of credit.

Student Loans:

You also need to consider student loans. You may be qualified for a student grant from the government. This is the first place you want to start before committing yourself to a loan agreement.

AVOIDING COMPLICATIONS FOR

HOMEOWNERS

Avoiding complications in credit repair is almost important as getting out of debt. When we have bills that were neglected simply because we didn't have the money to pay the bills, or else we purchased items instead of paying the bills, we are in debt.

If you are considering a Home Equity Loan to get out of your current mortgage...DON"T. Why? Simply because most Home Equity Loans get you deeper in debt and once you are obligated you will find the problem is more complicated than we you applied for the loan. Lenders often target home owners with financial difficulties offering them high interest rates and making them believe it is a solution for debt relief.

In most cases, this is where foreclosures come in, or selling homes come into place. The solution is only an option to get you in debt deeper. One solution then is for homeowners to consider the Reverse Mortgage Loans. This type of loan is often as equity against your home, belongings, and so on. The loan offers a 'cash advance' solution and requires that the owner does not pay on the mortgage until the end of the mortgage term or when the home is sold.

Most lenders provide a lump sum advance, a line of credit, or else a monthly installment to the home owners. Some lenders even offer a combination to the homeowners. This is certainly a good solution for repairing your credit, and building your credit to a new future. The downside is that Reverse Home Mortgage Loans often are more suitable for the older generation of people that have built equity over the years in their homes.

Another disadvantage is that almost all home loans require upfront payments, such as title, insurance, application fees, origination fees, interest and so on. Therefore, it pays to ask questions and shop around before taking out another loan to repair or build your credit. Fannie Mae Home Keeper Mortgage Programs are one of the many that offer a Reverse Home Mortgage Loan.

Another option for paying off your debts and repairing your credit is to borrow the money from family members or friends. If you have someone that trusts you enough to loan you the money to get out of debt, it is often better than getting a loan. There are several options or questions you must consider before asking family members or friends to loan you the money to build or repair your credit. One of those questions should be the obvious.

Can these people afford to lend me the money to get out of debt? Are these people kind enough to loan you money without putting high demands on you. Of course there may be interest involved, but remember they are loaning you money they could be spending on their own bills.

Is it possible that you can repay the loan without complicating your situation further?

Can I repay these people that loan me the money to free myself of one debt?

How long do I have to repay the loan?

Make sure there are no extra complications before asking friends or family for money to help get you out of debt. One of the best solutions for finding a way to repair your credit is searching the options to make the money yourself. If you have a mortgage payment and struggling each month to make ends meet, you might want to sell your home. Many homeowners go for this option simply because they make more money in the long run.

Once they sell their home they are often able to repay their mortgage loan and then take out a loan for another mortgage more affordable. If you decide to sell your home to repair your credit and get out of debt, be sure that you look around for the best possible solutions in order to prevent further complications.

Make sure you know how much is owed on your home before you set a price for resell. If there are any repairs that are minor or major, try to repair them first before selling. If you can't afford to repair the home, try to do minimal repair so that you can up the price of the home you are selling.
of the mortgage term on the mortgage or when your residence is sold.

AVOIDING CREDIT DECLINATIONS

Sorry you are declined...

Have you ever heard this before when you went to apply for a loan or a credit card?

If you have, this means that your credit files has some negative reports and it is time to clean up your act. Credit files are a report that contains your credit score and history. Three major companies hold your files and allow others to view them when you apply for a loan, credit report, job, apartment, and so on.

If that report or file has negative results you will hear...sorry you are declined. If you are declined then it is time to get started to rebuild your life. Credit bureaus obtain their information about you from all creditors that has done business with you. If you missed payments, ignored payments, or else simply overlooked payments the reports are sent to <u>TransUnion</u>, <u>Equifax</u> and <u>Experian</u> for review.

Once the bureau's has found negligence against you, your credit scores are immediately dropped. The lower your score means that you have fewer chances in life to get a loan, credit card, apartment, insurance, and so on. The higher your score means that you have opportunities to buy a new car, get a home mortgage loan or a major credit card from any source practically. The outlook for bad credit ratings then is something we want to reconstruct rather than ignore since it means our respect is in jeopardy. Many people around the world are filing bankruptcy, consulting with debt management programs, counselors, and other resources to find a solution to get out of debt.

The fact is these people are adding problems to their lives. When you apply for bankruptcy this stays on your credit file for 10 years and in some instances fifteen years. If you consult with debt management agencies or the wrong debt management counselors, you are only adding expenses rather than deducting bills. The law provides us a degree of protection, but the total outlook is that when we have bad credit we are walking on pins and needles for the rest of our lives unless we clean up our act.

Bad credit can lead to judgments against us, lawsuits, foreclosures, repossessions and so on. When we have bad credit we are subject to become homeless, broke, hungry and then some. The key then to success is to find a solution that works best for us. If you are working or even on Welfare or Disability it is possible to reestablish your credit. The first thing you have to do is make sure your living arrangements, vehicle, living necessities and so on are in accordance with your income.

If you are spending more than you are making the chances of you getting out of debt will decrease. On the other hand, if you monitor your income and spend within your means you may find a solution to get out of debt. You might also want to look into part-time jobs if you are on Welfare of on Disability. The sources allow you to make so much money each month.

You will still receive your checks with a little less income, but for the most part, it is a step in the right direction since you will be getting back on your own two feet. In addition, if you are working and making less than what you are worth you might want to find a higher paying job that could benefit your future. There are many options available to building your credit.

If you have a vehicle that is costing you more than you make, you might want to consider selling the vehicle and purchasing a used car. Used cars when maintenance is kept often last and are less expensive than newer vehicles. If you are paying more than you make on Mortgage you might want to consider selling your home, paying off your debts and work toward restoring your life.

To avoid declines it is important that you find a solution to repair your credit. Relying on others has proven in most cases to be nothing more than a waste of time. Therefore, the solution is finding what works for you.

AVOIDING PAYDAY LOANS

If you are trying to make ends meet and have past due bills, piling up the last resource is taking out a payday loan to pay your dues. There are many sources available today that offer payday advances. The loans are issued after you show proof of banking account, Social Security, Driver License and Pay stub proofs. This information is used against you, often the lenders will deduct money from your accounts including interest, and principals that apply to each loan you take out.

If you are applying for a payday loan online...Beware...Some of the sources are not even institutes that specialize in payday loans. When you are trying to repair your credit, the last thing you need to do is spend money that is not necessary.

When you borrow money from payday loaners, your personal information may not be private. Since many of the lenders are outside of the United States and are out of government regulations, your information just might fall into anyone's hands. This puts your credit at great risk. Payday loans offer you a loan against your paycheck, but the downside is your will be paying high fees for getting the loan.

Therefore, you are wasting money and taking a chance on your identity. If you are searching for help to repair your credit, it might be wise to search the market for legitimate resources that will help you restore your credit at little or no cost to you. There are Debt Counselors available that assist people with credit repair, but the best source is you. You might be wise to check out government options that are available to people with bad credit.

Many services are available help you to repair your life. The best solution is keeping up to date on your bills if possible or minimizing your monthly installments by opting for credit cards that have no fees attached and low interest rates. If you have a credit card, or else applying for a credit card avoid charging items to your cards unless it is absolutely necessary.

You might want to apply for a different credit card if you card has high interest rates and discontinue your old card once you receive your new card. If you suspect that someone has access to your card be sure to contact your provider immediately to report the card lost or stolen. Be sure to only provide your personal information to those you trust. Never give information pertaining to you freely. If you are considering a loan to pay off your debts check the market first before applying, since the more applications you fill out applies against your credit report. You might want to cut back on your utilities also to save funds that can be applied to your bills.

One way to cut back on electricity is by keeping all your plugs out of the socket if you are not using the appliance. When you have appliances or other items plugged into the outlets and nothing is used, it uses electricity. You may also want to cut back on gas mileage. Estimate your travel to work, stores, meetings, et cetera, and deduct any travel that leads nowhere.

You might even want to consider reducing your weekly grocery bill. Using coupons or buying items on sale is a sure way to put money in your pocket. Another helpful tip in saving money is to cut back on your entertainment expenses until your bills are paid in full.

Now if you want to make money you might consider selling items that are not needed in your home. Be sure to sell items of value to raise the funds to repair your credit. You might want to consider checking around the marketplace for lower insurance coverage on your home, car, or Life policies. Anytime you make the effort to reduce charges each month is an effort to getting on the road to repair.

Again, payday loans are not the answer and only cause more problems. If you are trying to get out of debt, 'resources' are the answer. Knowing the right resources takes time and effort on your part, but there is a solution for repairing credit.

INTERRUPTIONS IN BAD CREDIT

Building your credit after repeated interruptions is a constant headache we all want to avoid. There are many sources that will take full advantage of you when the opportunity arises. If you feel bad simply because you can't meet your bills expectations at the moment they arrive, then you are not alone.

The fact is, even the best of us are struggling to meet some expectation that the system has placed on us. We calculate weekly the amount we spend on groceries, which are constantly increasing, as well as other bills that are constantly on the rise. It seems at times it is a no win situation, but the fact is there is always a solution to most problems.

The problem most times is some of us do not have the means to find those solutions. This brings forth more stress and often we feel that we are alone. If you trying to build your credit status you need to find the resources that can help you get results. The marketplace offers credit repair kits, which can lead us in the right direction to repairing credit, but the disadvantage is that many of the kits are expensive.

Let's face it, not everyone has the money to spend on commodities that claim to help us. Some of us struggle harder than others just to survive. Life is forever changing and in order to keep up with the changes we all have to find a solution. Therefore, I am going to tell you where you can get a free credit repair kit. Your local library stores a wealth of information and it is free to the public.

In most libraries that have credit repair kits, credit repair books, or debt management solution books. Anything you want at your disposal and it is all free information. The library also has copy and fax machines often, and if you notice in the credit repair guide or kit, it will have copies of the letters you can write to your creditors. Make yourself some copies and once you fill them out as instructed, you are on your way to repairing your credit.

The library also has guides or kits for filing bankruptcy. If you do not see a way out, then you may want to go this route. In most cases, you can do a Pro Bono Bankruptcy, which means you will represent yourself in the courtroom. I just wanted to let you know that if you file a <u>Chapter 7 Bankruptcy</u>, you will have monthly installments to make, but if you file Chapter 13 Bankruptcy then the courts wipe out all your debts.

The problem is that bankruptcies remain on credit files for up to ten years or longer. If you can avoid bankruptcy do so, however it is not the end of the world if you do. I know people personally that filed bankruptcy and was able to get loans for mortgage, cars and so on. If you know what you are, doing you can do anything no matter how bad your situation is. Avoid Debt Consolidation, simply because it is means you will be paying fees and costs to others to get out of debt, which only adds up the bills. You might want to consider a Debt Counselor from a respected organization.

It makes sense to check out any business first before spending money or asking for services. The BBB offers free information on organizations, businesses and corporations. Once you have investigated the service then you will know if the people are really trying to help you. Any service that tells you they can get you out of debt in no time at all is pulling your leg. The fact is even when you pay your bills your credit will continue to list all the bad debts, it will only say after the debt listed...Resolved.

Finally message while I am thinking about it. It is important to get copies of your credit reports from TransUnion, Equifax, and Experian. You can find any information you need online. Knowing your status in life is the beginning of repairing bad credit.

USING BARTERING SYSTEM TO RESTORE

YOUR CREDIT

Restoring Credit is Essential for surviving in today's time. Today's barter is moving back to the system as many people including business owners find it to be a solution for getting out debt or expanding their company. This might sound crazy, but if you think about it you can find a way to make money.

Barter means to exchange goods or services for equal value. However in some cases you can find people willing to exchange goods or services for less value. Bartering could even mean changing products or items for money. For example, if you have a bunch of Video games or a game system and in debt it might be wise to sell your game system and games, or trade it for something of more value to resell.

Some people out their want something that you have but can't afford it and are willing to exchange items for what they are wanting. If you can get a better deal to raise money how much easier can it get. If you have a lot of items in your home you can also sell your items on eBay, including the barter exchanges that you obtained. Reselling items to raise money to repair your credit might be the only solution available at times. Once you get into bartering and reselling you might find it an interest source for making money and start your own business.

The stars are at your limit. Be sure that you don't invest money into items that are not going to produce revenue. You could also raise money to repair your business if you have access to the Internet and can write. If you have good English skills it is possible to generate a small amount of income to make ends meet. Don't think that this is an alternative to work, rather keep your job and do your writing on the sidelines.

Most of the buyers on the market pay very little for articles, but in some cases you can make a lump sum that can pay off your bills. Credit repair is a job in itself. When you are trying to restore your credit it takes effort on your part. It also takes thinking since we often have to search for a solution to find a way out of debt.

There are many ways to generate money to repay bills. One way to generate money is to cut back on expenses. This is not as good as finding a barter system or selling system that will generate more income, but hey it works. One of the bartering systems that stuck out in my mind is when a woman told me about exchanging stickers, stationary, and other similar items.

The woman was able to generate a small amount of income, at the same time exchanging her ideas over the Internet. If you are able to connect to the Internet you might want to do a search to find out which services are available that can offer you a source of income that can get you on your feet.

The Internet is swarming with Spam so be very carefully before making a decision. Some services offer a small fee to get you a training package to help you start selling. eBay has a great package for $29.95, but be sure that you can market and sale before you commit yourself.

Another solution maybe trading your car for a more expensive vehicle and resell the car to pay off your creditors... This can happen believe it or not, but there are people out there that want something new and willing to downgrade to get the change. The world is filled with people of all sorts and sometimes we can get real good deals that can benefit us.

Regardless of your situation there is always a solution to survive and get out of debt. It makes no sense to rely on services and business that will only take your money, when there are options that can put you right into business while repairing your credit at the same time. Barter credit repair makes no sense until you come up with the solution for making money on your exchanges and using the money to repay your debts.

be an alternate instead keep your work to work and do your own writing.

BILLS ARE DUE AND CREDIT REPAIR IS IN PLACE

The bills are due and credit repair is in place. This happens too many times with many individuals and families, so don't get discouraged there is hope. We can calculate our bills by factoring in utilities, telephone, credit cards, mortgage, rent, lease, purchases, and so on. Each of us needs a vehicle to get to work so this is obviously an important item that we need. Vehicles are used or new.

So you need to ask if you need a new car or a used car. If you already have car payments is there a solution for lowering your monthly payments? Telephone and utilities bills can often wait a while longer before the services are disconnected, so if you have a late car payment it might be wise to take care of this loan first. This will give you time to find a solution for making payments on your phone and utilities. You might even want to check into some of the savings that utilities and phone companies offer.

Savings such as Senior Citizen Discounts, or low-income family discounts are often available by many of the providers. Try to keep minimal services on your phone to avoid overpaying a phone bill. If the service providers offer a lower rate on packages it might be wiser to go this route, instead of adding features separately. If your funds are low and you are not making enough to make ends meet, there are organizations available that help low-income families make ends meet.

The Social Services offer help to families with low-income, and often will help pay utility bills. There is help available you just have to be willing to ask for the help. If you are confined to a high car payment and see that you can't make ends meet, you might want to sell the vehicle to pay off your loan. Try to resell the car for a higher price that what is owed to make a little extra cash. Lenders sometimes offer extension on car payments so you do have the option of calling your lender and asking for help.

Some lenders will even offer a new payment agreement to reduce your monthly installments. When you see that you are having difficulty with paying what you owe, it is always wise to come up with the best possible solution. Researching the market is a great source for finding a solution to repairing credit. The key is being careful and smart when you find that source.

Never assume that any company that claims to lower your bills and help repair your credit works. It is easier to get in debt than it is to get out of debt, so when you make any purchases or sign your name to a debt make sure that you can meet the expectations placed on you. We all go through situations that make times difficult at some point; however there is always a way to get out. Loans that require collateral upfront are often some of the loans that are difficult to escape. For example, if you apply for a loan and put your car up as collateral, the company will probably repossess your vehicle if you continue missing payments.

On the other hand if you purchase a refrigerator on credit the lender most likely will not confiscate your item; however the lender will most likely take you to court for payment. This only adds problem to problem, so if you can avoid loans with collateral, by all means do so. If your credit isn't so bad that you can't take out another loan to repay your current debts, this is another solution to repairing your credit.

For example, you owe $7000 and take out a loan for $10,000. If you repay your debts, you have $3000 remaining which you can use to pay down the current loan. This will help you repair your credit and build your credit ratings. Make sure you find a lender that will offer low interest rates and low monthly installments so that you can make ends meet. If you are able to get the loan don't hesitate to repay all your debts rather than spending the money on other items.

CHAPTER 3 – CREDIT BUILDING IDEAS AND STRATEGIES

If you have delinquent credit and are married, you might want to build your credit in your name instead of using your spouse. Somebody has to have stability. Also if you are divorced and all the credit cards of credit information are in your spouse's name you will need to re-establish your credit in your name. Getting your credit re-established is the first step to repairing your credit.

When you obtain your credit report you will see that your spouse's name is listed on the credit reports. This is because together you and your spouse applied for credit cards, took out car loans or what have you. This means that you are responsible for your spouse's account. The advantage is that credit bureaus cannot list the negative accounts against you if you are divorced. Once you have copies of your credit report you will then need to cancel all joint accounts. If you contact the creditors to resolve the issues on your credit report is sure to ask the creditors to take in consideration your spouse's credit history.

It is important to bring into light your spouse's credit history when applying for a loan. Let the lenders know that you are now divorced and starting your own credit line. If you apply for credit cards, be sure the cards are in your name and use them wisely since this helps to rebuild your credit quicker than most sources. Make sure that you pay minimum balance on the credit card accounts each month to avoid delinquencies. If at all possible when you see that your funds are low; pay your bills rather than making a purchase on your credit card.

Once you bills are paid be sure to make a payment on your credit card. This method not only keeps you out of trouble with other creditors, but offers a solution for repairing your credit. If you can afford to pay your bills each month and use your credit card be sure to only purchase items you need and keep it at a minimal. If at all possible payoff your credit card balances each month to avoid interest.

Interest rates cost an additional hundreds of dollars in the long run, so paying off your dues on time can save you money. If you don't have credit cards and decide to choose a card is honest on your application and look for the best interest rates available. If you are in debt it is wise to pay off your dues before applying for a credit card, unless you intend to use the card to get out of debt. If you plan to use the card to get out of debt search for the best interest rates, as well as cards that offer cash back on your spending.

There are tips for managing credit cards to repair credit. It is important that you are consistent with the use of your name. For example, if your name is Robert Leon Swisher Jr., always sign your name accordingly. Do not use your card dishonestly for advantages. Few people believe that lying can get them out of a problem. The truth lying gets you in deeper. If you are filling out an application for credit cards tell the truth.

It is important that you understand the timeframe to apply for a credit card. If you are out of work, lived at your resident for less than a year or you have negatives on your credit report, this is not a good time to apply for a credit card. If you are stable it is always wise to apply with lenders where you have done business with them at a later time. Building your credit after divorce is difficult at times.

However it is not an impossible task. It is important that you are aware that most credit card solicitations are gimmicks that only offer you a solution for hanging yourself. Instead of getting out a rope, it is wise to stay alert, and investigate any credit card offer made available to you.

Finally, you want to avoid low introductory rates on credit cards since after about six months the interest rates often hit the roof.

CAUTION YOU NEED TO OBSERVE WHEN BUILDING

YOUR CREDIT

Building credit can be a really exciting thing. Avenues of opportunities can be found should you do it correctly. It's crucial to steer clear of. Scammers available on the market these days are benefiting from people in disarray. It's necessary that you be careful. Simply take every step prior to making a choice, and think about all your choices. It can be hard to choose which one to take care of, Whenever you have lenders making supplies. Follow these tips coping with a creditor and when picking on: The rate of interest will apply on all payments that are minimal. A good example is below:

Q1. What interest rate are they offering?

Any firm that doesn't advise you or let is a fraud. In many places, lots of the businesses are banned Underneath the Federal Laws and often lots of them work agreements out to get forward. There is legit organizations and businesses which may help you reestablish your credit for little if any charge. Assessing the market is the ideal solution for finding the ideal sources. The regional library has a plethora of information at your disposal and it's totally free to sift through the web pages. Make the most of any opportunity that presents itself and you are on your way to creating your credit score.

Response: The rate of interest on your credit card plays a part in your ability. When at all possible make payment. Remember that creating payment might not be possible. That is the reason you have to think about the interest rate which you're agreeing to. Don't turn into the next sucker!!!

The interest rate will apply on all minimum payments. An example is below:

Balance owed on account : $350.00
Interest Rate   : 5.7% (.057)
Minimum Payment   : $19.95

Think about this, $19.95 only pays for the interest that is going to be added to the balance owed. You may think that you can subtract $19.95 from the $350.00 owed, however, do not forget to add the .057 to the balance. Your balance will go and continue to collect interest.

Q2. Make your payments in time.

Response: don't make a payment after 45 days of your payment and Don't make payments until 30 days of the payment. After 45 days are considered 8, payments received before 30 days receive a review by 21, and obligations made.

Q3. Don't use over 3 times per year.

Response: If you're doing, you can be denied credit because these activities are perceived as searching for credit. If you're suspected of buying for credit, you will be denied by your lenders. You may keep an eye on the number of times you have applied for credit and with that by taking a look at your credit report. Your credit report reveals of the individuals have asked for the previous two decades into your account. After two decades, the list drops off your own report. Take it slow As soon as you start paying a creditor. You will find many offers and it's very tempting to take all of them up.

Q4. Keep all your receipts and contracts

Response: Keep all your receipts for payments. Lenders have been proven to misplace a payment let us hope it is not yours. Rest assured if it's, giving you kept your receipts. Saving your contract together with no creditor is advised. In the event a dispute should arise, the creditor will make certain to throw in remarks regarding signature and your agreement to the contract.

The issue to do to your own credit with respect is enjoy it, protect, respect and particularly take pride. Having good credit will extend the horizons of chance for you and your future supplying your pursue your own credit and is a luxury.

BUILDING CREDIT AND STOPPING CREDITORS

Building your credit is a sure-fired solution for stopping creditors and collection agencies from nagging you every day. If you are attempting to reestablish your status in life, you must realize there is a bumpy road ahead. Creditors are people you owe and if you do not pay, the creditors will go lengths to get their money.

Regardless of the laws and regulations stipulated on credit bureaus, creditors, collection agencies, and other sources that collect debt, many will break all the laws, simply because they want their money. Money has been the root of all humankind evil and when it comes to money, everybody wants some. The best solution to stopping creditors and collection agencies ahead of the game is to pay those bills on time. If you have utilities, insurance policies, car payments, mortgages, credit cards, and other debts you might want to layout a budget plan that you can meet each month.

Combining all your payments will help you see where dangers lurk. If you see, any potential risks ahead make sure to find a solution ahead of the game to avoid creditors and collection agency hassles. No one likes it when people nag us, but when we owe money, you can bet your last dollar nagging is in the making. Do not bite off more than you can chew. If you see that, you are in debt deeper than you thought do not go out to the department stores and shop until you drop.

This will only make matters worse and you are risking your home, car, and other assets in the process. If you see that you are in over your head or potential risks could develop, you might want to get ahead by selling a few valuable items. When you are paid for, the items make sure you apply the funds to your bills, or else open a savings account that will benefit you and your money. Savings that offer no start up fees or interest against your money is the best solution for saving cash. If you get money back or interest on your money in the bank, how much better, you are making money.

Money is what makes the world go around, so if you can make money you will have a solution for building your credit. The last thing you want is escalating to a debt you can get out of and having creditors call you daily. After creditors calls, then you will get calls from collection agencies. After the two are done torturing you mentally, you will have to deal with lawyers, judges, and other potential threatening personnel.

I point this out because many people do not realize the severity of ignoring their bills. If you have a good credit standing currently, it is wise to get copies of your credit reports from the three B's. Keeping your file on hand and current can help you to monitor your credit scores. If you notice any activity on your report that is against you and you did not agree to the debt, it is important to contact the credit bureaus immediately. Your credit is in all aspects of the word your life. If you have bad credit you can be turned down from a job, denied a rental, or turned down when you apply for any line of credit. If you have bad credit you might as well blackball today.

There is hope however if you have bad credit. Government agencies and private institutes are teaming up to help those of us with bad credit. The impossible has happen, because now even if your credit is bad you can get a loan, a home, car, or even a credit card. Pre-paid cards are available to those with bad credit. Pre-paid cards are the same in contrast as major credit cards, only you apply money to the account, paying a low fee and then you can use the card.

The world is starting to recognize the struggles that happen every day for many families and individuals, the best solution however for stopping creditors is to build your credit by paying those bills. Never give up hope!

BUILDING CREDIT HISTORY

Building your credit is a sure-fired solution for stopping creditors and collection agencies from nagging you every day. If you are attempting to reestablish your status in life, you must realize there is a bumpy road ahead. Creditors are people you owe and if you do not pay, the creditors will go lengths to get their money.

Regardless of the laws and regulations stipulated on credit bureaus, creditors, collection agencies, and other sources that collect debt, many will break all the laws, simply because they want their money. Money has been the root of all humankind evil and when it comes to money, everybody wants some. The best solution to stopping creditors and collection agencies ahead of the game is to pay those bills on time. If you have utilities, insurance policies, car payments, mortgages, credit cards, and other debts you might want to layout a budget plan that you can meet each month.

Combining all your payments will help you see where dangers lurk. If you see, any potential risks ahead make sure to find a solution ahead of the game to avoid creditors and collection agency hassles. No one likes it when people nag us, but when we owe money, you can bet your last dollar nagging is in the making. Do not bite off more than you can chew. If you see that, you are in debt deeper than you thought do not go out to the department stores and shop until you drop.

This will only make matters worse and you are risking your home, car, and other assets in the process. If you see that you are in over your head or potential risks could develop, you might want to get ahead by selling a few valuable items. When you are paid for, the items make sure you apply the funds to your bills, or else open a savings account that will benefit you and your money. Savings that offer no start up fees or interest against your money is the best solution for saving cash. If you get money back or interest on your money in the bank, how much better, you are making money.

Money is what makes the world go around, so if you can make money you will have a solution for building your credit. The last thing you want is escalating to a debt you can get out of and having creditors call you daily. After creditors calls, then you will get calls from collection agencies. After the two are done torturing you mentally, you will have to deal with lawyers, judges, and other potential threatening personnel.

I point this out because many people do not realize the severity of ignoring their bills. If you have a good credit standing currently, it is wise to get copies of your credit reports from the three B's. Keeping your file on hand and current can help you to monitor your credit scores. If you notice any activity on your report that is against you and you did not agree to the debt, it is important to contact the credit bureaus immediately. Your credit is in all aspects of the word your life. If you have bad credit you can be turned down from a job, denied a rental, or turned down when you apply for any line of credit. If you have bad credit you might as well blackball today.

There is hope however if you have bad credit. Government agencies and private institutes are teaming up to help those of us with bad credit. The impossible has happen, because now even if your credit is bad you can get a loan, a home, car, or even a credit card. Pre-paid cards are available to those with bad credit. Pre-paid cards are the same in contrast as major credit cards, only you apply money to the account, paying a low fee and then you can use the card.

The world is starting to recognize the struggles that happen every day for many families and individuals, the best solution however for stopping creditors is to build your credit by paying those bills. Never give up hope!

BAD CREDIT BUILDING CREDIT

If you have, bad credit gets a **DO-IT-YOURSELF-Kit** and gets the balls rolling. You can go to your public library and get books that will guide you through the steps of repairing your credit. Most libraries allow you to copy and print forms that you must fill out and then send to your credits.

There are systematic guides at your local library that has the tools for instructor debtors how to write letters to creditors. Letters are probably better than phoning creditors, since some creditors could care less about your situation and may threaten you. Another good reason for writing letters is that (copy in writing) is more valuable in a courtroom than a conversation on the phone. If something is said or an agreement is reached and the creditor later denies his or her claims then you can present this to any courtroom and they will listen to you first.

Any documents that pertain to your credit history should be stored in a safe area. If you send letters to your creditors keep a copy of each letter sent and store it in a safe area. If you notice any errors on your bills or credit, reports make sure that you contact the appropriate professionals and dispute the charges immediately. If you have credit cards and used the card to purchase an item or use a service and this person sold you a defected item or else provided bad service, you DO NOT have to make payment toward the charges.

You do however have to dispute the charges with the services or stores that sold you the product or service. If the sources refuse to give you an item usable, or else reimburse you for a service or product you have the right to deny payment.

Once you have disputed the charges with the sources you will then contact your card provider and let them know what occurred. If you are lucky enough to have a credit card with bad credit, use the card to repay your debts and then meet the monthly installments on the credit card each month. Ironically, you are getting out of debt while going in debt deeper. It is a solution when all else false.

In other words, if you use the card to pay your debts each month and then payoff your credit cards the following month and then turnaround and uses the card to pay that month bills....

Now you see where I am going. Credit cards have interest rates so the bills each month on the card will increase.

No, Credit...No Problem

I do not need a credit line or credit card; I pay all my bills each month with money. Is this you?

Well then, you have the obvious answer, but what if...

In today's world, we are moving into an era that requires us to have at least one major credit card. When you phone any business where you have debts, they will first ask you to pay with a credit card. If you go apply for a job, apartment, mortgage, car loan, or any other credit line you most likely will get a rejection notice in the mail.

Most lenders will not give credit to anyone that has no credit history.

The reason is that we are expected to establish a credit line when we are teens, and if we do not the lenders are often suspicious. The lenders do not have an idea and can only base their judgments of you on assumptions.

Can I assume this person will make monthly payments on time?

Has this person taken for granted a loan from a friend or family member in the past and there are no records available for me to see if it is true?

There are many reasons that lenders will refuse you a loan if you do not have a credit history. The best solution is starting up a line of credit now, pay off your dues on time and avoid making purchases on items you do not really need. Staying out of debt means regulating your money each month and paying your bills on time.

BUILDING CREDIT PREVENTING REPAIR

If you want to prevent credit repair procedures, you need to keep your payments up to date. Financial emergencies may come up, so it is important that you meet minimal payments on time. If you have utilities, house payment, car payment, or other dues try to knock them out to avoid complications. If you are in debt over your head and have very little income and assets it might be wise to do nothing, Sounds insane, but the reality is when you are taking to court most of the collectors won't be able to collect a dime.

This procedure is called '*judgment proof.*' If you elect this procedure you won't go to jail. There are advantages by acting on the 'judgment proof,' such as the Federal Laws protect you against creditors coming to your home and confiscating your belongings. The downside is you are not resolving anything and in the long run you won't get credit.

On the other hand if you want to face your credit problems, you can take several steps to build your credit. If you have an attitude "it doesn't matter how much I owe, I am in debt and can't get out." Then you probably should take the 'judgment proof' method. However, if you have an attitude "How much do I owe so I can work to resolve." Then you are on the road to rebuilding your credit. Start by over viewing the current bills that you have received.

You can also call the companies that sent you the bill to find out how much you owe. Once you have totaled your bills, and find an amount that you can pay each month toward all the bills owed. You can also get reports of your credit report from TransUnion, Equifax, and Experian, however unless you have recently applied for a loan and was turned down you won't get these reports free. You can go online to check out the various sources that offer credit reports, and some places enable you to get all three reports for around $25. This is wise since the more you apply for loans or any source of credit, the more it goes against your credit score. The credit score is more important than the rating.

When it comes to dealing with credit repair or credit building, we have several options available. If you are in debt for more than $10,000 and your future doesn't look promising, you can always file bankruptcy. Be alert that bankruptcy doesn't necessary mean that you are out of debt, rather it means that the courts will decide on a monthly fee that you can afford to repay your debts.

Some debts are dropped in bankruptcies, depending on your lawyer and what he/she can do for you. You could also apply for a consolidation loan, which is a little better than bankruptcy in the sense you promise to the lenders that you will pay a certain amount each month until the debts are paid in full. It pays to shop around if you are going this route, since some lenders charges fees to get you out of debt, as well as some lenders do not work hard to get you affordable monthly installments for repayments.

The last thing you need is to be paying more than you can afford each month. If you have assets, such as a house or car, you might want to sell to raise money to get out of debt. This almost always works out in your best interest. If you can't afford payments in the first place, you have nothing to lose. Once you sell your item then you can pay off any other debts you may have and work toward building your credit.

The more effort you make in building your credit, the more

opportunities you will have of reestablishing your credit rating and score. If you are struggling to get out of debt be sure to set up a budget for yourself so that you are not going in deeper. When you are in debt small sacrifices or even big sacrifices needs to happen in order to repair and rebuild your credit score and ratings.

CREDIT BUILDING STRATEGIES

IF you are attempting to build your credit there are many strategies we can look at to help you get started. If you have no credit, bad credit or good credit, building credit is important since regardless of your situation, you do not want to go down.

Strategies for Building Credit:

If you do not have any credit at all, you will need to start somewhere. One strategy for building credit is to apply for a credit card or a personal loan and ask your family members or friends to co-sign the application. Once you have opened an account, make sure you meet all monthly obligations, since if you miss any payments at all your co-signer is responsible. If you do not have a credit history, you might want to opt for credit cards issued by gas stations, or else open an account with a department store.

These cards are relatively easy to get hold of, and it helps you to build credit. After you established some line of credit, make your payments faithfully and after about six months you will be entitled to more credit. It is not recommended, but if you have a personal loan and still paying after six months, you might want to take out a loan to repay this loan and start payment on the other loan. I recommend this since it can free the co-signer from responsibility. Never take out more than you need when applying for a loan and always check the interest rates and upfront fees to avoid overpaying.

Bad Credit Strategy:

If you have bad credit and want to restore or build your credit, you must first start by sending for copies of your credit reports. The reports are free once per year and can be obtained by <u>TransUnion</u>, <u>Equifax</u> and <u>Experian</u>. After you have reviewed your reports make sure no activities are listed against you that is not your own. If you notice, any actions on your report immediately write the three bureaus and ask for an investigation.

Once you have disputed your report, the next step is knocking down each account until your credit is clear. If you are struggling with money, you might want to knock out the secured debts first and then work through the unsecured debts. It may take some time but you will see results after your debts are paid in full. A great strategy for those of us in debt is to save money each month and apply it to our dues. If you are spending money, for entertainment give it up for now and get out of debt.

Many things in life are free of charge and often fun and exciting. Remember when you make sacrifices something rewarding always returns. Another helpful strategy is pulling out all your resources. If you have skills, you might want to open a small business and use those skills to the fullest. You will make money and build your credit.

Killing many birds with one stone is the saying that works best when you learn what it means. It is also wise to cut back on expenses when you owe are your credit is bad. If you are spending money you do not have, it is only sending you backwards. There are many strategies for getting back on your feet again. One great strategy is to avoid missing car payments.

Good Credit Scores:

Finally, if you have a good credit score you want to strategize to maintain this score or else elevate the score. If your credit is good, you want to continue the budget that is obviously working and work toward increasing your income to make sure you meet all payments each month. The last thing you need to do is apply for additional lines of credit if you already have credit established.

Payoff what you owe now and buy what you want later. One of the biggest mistakes many of us make is taking for granted our situation. If we have a lot of money and a great line of credit, we often go on spending binges. This is ludicrous and is a defected strategy that buries us in quicksand.

Building Credit in Despair

Building credit can lead to despair if you do not know where to get started. Creditors come in all forms and some of them are out to take you for a road, so this alone makes the struggle increase. If you have bad credit or no credit then you know how difficult it is to get ahead. Sometimes it may seem the more you try the harder it gets. In fact, this is sometimes true simply because too many people lack knowledge when it comes to building or repairing credit.

Many people will take the wrong path when they are trying to build or repair their credit and this often leads to a bigger struggle. If you are in search of a solution to repair or build, your credit the first thing you will need to do is get in contact with reality. The fact is if you have no credit or bad credit the world is on your shoulders and it will take you to get them rascals off your back.

Credit is essential nowadays and nearly every business asks for a major credit card. If you do not have, credit established or else your credit is bad then you are in trouble when they say, "*all we accept are major credit cards.*" The world has gone mad. Instead of giving you a job when your credit is bad to help you get back on your feet again, they will often turn you down. This is insane, but it is the way the world operates. When you apply for a loan to get out of debt you will also get turned down in most cases.

The lenders figure since you did not pay your first debts you probably will not pay your new debts. Lenders rarely take into consideration that your situation is temporarily and could change at any time. When you do not have credit, few lenders do not assume that best possible option, rather they assume that you are a mishap in life. There are a few exceptions, but for the most part lenders look down on your when you have no credit at all or your credit is bad.

If your credit is bad, you might want to get started paying on your bills right away to repair your credit and get out of despair. If you do not have credit, it is time to start building for a better future as soon as possible. Instead of taking out a loan or else applying for a credit card on your own, you might want to take a trustworthy friend or family member.

Taking a friend or family member with you will come in handy when the lenders say, "*do you have a co-signer.*" After you are approved for a loan or credit card, make sure that you pay your bills on time to avoid defaults on your credit files as well as avoiding enemies. If you miss payments, the friend or family member that co-signed your contract is obligated to pay your dues. This all sounds crazy if you think about. People every day are filing bankruptcy, suffering debt issues, and so on, yet the system requires us to establish credit at an early age in life to stay up with the Smith and Jones.

The system is set up to get you one-way or the other. Therefore, if you are building credit for the first time makes sure that you do not overdo yourself. If you are purchasing a car, make sure you know what you are getting into to avoid future debt issues. If you are purchasing a car, consider a car that is inexpensive and economical to avoid overpaying for a fancy car that will only last for a short time.

None of us really needs a Mercedes Benz, but some of us can afford it.

If you can afford a Mercedes and know that your future is prosperous by all means, apply for the loan. On the other hand, if you see that your future is shaky and you do not have the funds to support an outrageous lifestyle, then go for the Bug it is cheaper and it will save you despair in your future.

Building Credit to a Better Future

Building credit is building a better future. Nowadays it takes good credit scores to purchase a home, buy a car, and get a credit card and so on. If your credit is bad usually more bad follows. It takes you to find a solution to repair your credit.

The first step in repairing your credit is to take a look at each bill, including your past due bills. Make sure the current bills are paid in full if possible to avoid any more reporting on your credit report. Once you have taken care of your current bills work toward paying off your late bills.

Some current bills such as utilities or other unsecured bills can wait longer than others, so you might want to pay off your secured bills first. Secured bills means that you have more to lose so you want to take care of those first before paying off nonessential bills and risking losing your home, car or whatever you are paying on. Most utility companies will wait on a bill if you don't have the funds. You may be able to get some help paying utilities.

The Social Services and some Religious Organizations offer support to low-income families. If you have a loan with a bank you might want to contact your lender to see if there are options for reducing your monthly mortgage or car payments. Some banks are waiting for financial burdens to occur and offer a solution, such as refinancing your home or car.

You want to be careful since some of the loans have high interest rates attached. Some loans may even have hidden charges attached so it makes sense to read the fine prints thoroughly so that you are not taking advantage of. Remember you are attempting to repair your credit so finding the best deals is important. This brings us to cut backs. When we are striving to repair our credits we want to cut back on spending as much as possible. Sometimes we have to do without in order to better our future.

Credit repair is the process of building your credit history and reestablishing your life. This process means that you have to look at all angles to find a solution to repair your credit. When you are searching those angles you need to consider all aspects of what the solutions include. If there are added charges you probably are getting in deeper rather than building a better future and repairing your credit.

Debt Counselors, Deb Consolidation, Bankruptcy and other companies that offer credit repair solutions are often the last resort to repairing credit. Even if you think bankruptcy is the answer you must realize you will need a few hundred dollars upfront to start the process.

Lawyers are not cheap!

On top of the high prices you will have to pay you will also go through court proceedings as well as many other headaches. Therefore if you can find a way out of debt on your own this is the best solution. If you are in over your head and have nothing to lose it might be wise to ignore your debts.

This sounds ludicrous but if you can't get out this sometimes is the only answer to debt relief. If you are on the spot and not so deep in debt you might ask your family or friends for a loan, only enough to pay off your debts. You might have to pay interest, but friends and family will often charge less and give you a longer time frame to repay your debt. The solution is often better than applying for a loan to pay off your debts from a bank.

Most lenders at bank are welcoming people that are struggling and take full advantage by finding you a loan with high interest rates. Your monthly installments are often lower, but your price in the end is steep. It makes sense to search all options before deciding which solution for repairing your credit is right for you. Always keep in mind when you are repairing credit that you are working toward a better future.

Cooperation Credit Repair

When you are trying to get out of debt, you will need cooperation from others as well as yourself. If both of the sources are hard headed, I promise you your credit repair scheme will probably not work. Debt is an everyday part of life and we all have an obligation in life, and this includes both debtor and creditor. When you are dealing with creditors the first thing you want to do is cooperate as much as possible.

Most creditors are ready to work out an arrangement with you to help you stay on your feet. However, there are some creditors, which could care less about your situation and will avoid cooperation at all cost. If you run into this type of situation, by law you can report the representative, and ask to speak with his or her supervisor. According to the law, no one has the right to violate you whether it is speech, action, or other source.

You have the right to demand cooperation and understanding. If the representative disregards you when you ask to speak with the supervisor, simply hang up the phone and call back. My advice is to send the creditors a letter of recognition, letting them know you owe the debt and is currently working out a solution to resolve the issue. If possible, send a check for as little as $10, or whatever you can afford.

This will stay the creditors from sending your information to the collection agencies. It is important to act immediately on late bills before they do hit the collection agencies. The collection agencies are much more complex to deal with than common creditors. If you are in debt and find that you only have enough money to make ends meet, you might want to look into a few options available to you. If you have a family, single family, or individual you may qualify for a government loan or grant.

While applying for the loan or grant make sure, you stall the creditors until you get the loan or grant offered. Many debtors believe it is impossible to get out of debt once they go down. The truth is, there is always a way out of any situation practically. Giving up is the only way that your credit repair system will fail?

The only true failure in life is failure itself and this is a result of slackers, procrastinators, and quitters. If you need help with credit repair and do not know where to get started, you might want to search your mind.

Once you are finished with your search you will probably see, a resource and a solution that will help you find a way through repairing your credit. Your local library for example has a wealth of information that covers nearly every subject.

What about your local social services, do they have a resource available?

Community Action is another bridge you could cross when you can't find the answers to your credit repair in the areas you searched. I guarantee you will find some sort of information at your public library that will guide you through the steps of credit repair. The keyword "credit repair' is all you need to go through channel of communication that will lead you to repair.

The most important thing you want to remember when it comes to repairing your credit, or your credit period, is to never trust anyone that tells you they have all the answers. The market is swarming with bandits that are ready to take you for a ride. Spammers, Rammers, Crammers, and other types of predators are out there, so be careful. Those darn credit cards that tell you regardless of your credit history we will offer you a line of credit, is a crock.

In addition anyone that can tell you can get out of debt in 3 minutes, 16-36 days and so on is full of it. The truth is your score rises once you pay your debt, but the overall debts that you owed will remain faithful on that file until the three-seven-or ten-year period that the law allows. So open up that cooperation kit and get to rolling on your credit repair.

Chapter 4 -Creditors Calling it's Time to Repair your Credit

When the creditors are ringing the phone off the wall you know it is time to repair your credit. The United States alone has over millions of individuals and families struggling to find a way out of debt. This is why when you go online you see thousands of web sites that say they have the solution for relieving debt.

Don't be fooled!

Many of the telemarketers that claim they can get you out of debt can only bring forth more problems. There is no answer for all of us, but there is an answer for us all individually. Let's take a look at an example. Ok, you make $210 each week per paycheck. Your debt is around $5000 and you can't seem to see a way out. Now let's say you have two vehicles both are paid in full, and a monthly rent that equals $400. We know that you only have $640 per month to purchase food, pay utilities, clothes, and other items needed to survive.

We can't forget the phone bill. This sounds like an impossible situation, but in reality there is an answer available. Now if you phone bill is around $90 per month and you spent around $50 per week on groceries and around $150 per month on utilities. Be time you are finished adding this up you will see that you don't have a dime left at the end of the month. Therefore the solution is finding a job that pays more, searching for a low-income apartment that basis the rent on your income and using less utilities per month.

In today's time you will spend $50 easily on groceries and not get enough to make it to the next week. Therefore is it possible you can eat foods that are less expensive and last longer? When you are poor you got to live like a poor person. The sadness about people that are struggle is they often envy or strive to purchase items they don't really need. Instead of paying the bills on time, they often pay a portion of the bill and buy things that are not needed. If you have two cars and a single individual it is wise to sell one of the cars and apply the balance toward the bills.

You can see from this deduction that more money is needed to survive.

Why are you paying $400 for rent when there are many sources available that offer you rent for less?

Now let's turn this around.

What if you successfully rented a low-income apartment?

Let's say that your amount is reduced to $200 per month. This leaves you an extra $200 per month to pay utilities, buy groceries, pay insurance on one car, pay your phone bill, and have a couple of bucks left over each month. This is one solution and it doesn't bring forth much, but it does bring forth a small reward. Now if you can reduce your utilities to around $100 per month that is another $50 you could spend on bills. If your credit history is delinquent, yet you are not swarming in quicksand you might be eligible for a credit card.

The solution is not to get the card to buy items, rather it is to get a card that will help you make your monthly bills and allow you room to repay. Make sure the card has low interest rates and there are no annual fees attached. If you can get by without a credit card at all it will be better, but the fact is it is nearly impossible now to go without a credit card. If you can get a job that pays more for your work then this is helpful too.

The downside is when people get better paying jobs that often take it for granted and land deeper in debt. The more money you make the more you will spend. It pays to be careful with your money and stay alert to your credit situation to keep a repair in place. When creditors are calling it is time to repair your credit, so get ahead of the game before the phone rings.

Avoid Going To Court

If you ever entered a courtroom, you know that the stress elevates, even if you are in the room for someone else. Courts are an automatic source for lifting stress. Moreover, to avoid the courts means we have to abide by laws and pay our debts. If you have taking out a home mortgage, car loan, personal loan, or any other type of credit loan in some instances when the loans requirements are not meet you can be subpoenaed to court.

There are several courts that handle cases that involved negligence, starting with small claims court and finally judgment courts. Any courtroom is stressful, and many of the courts will look at both cases objectionable. However, the party involved in negligence is often deemed untrustworthy. If you want to avoid more stress than what you will endure on bad credit reports, it is important to make wise decisions before spending money you do not have.

To avoid court judgments, liens or lawsuits it is important to meet payments on your monthly installments. If you find an area of your life when you see that it will be difficult to meet demands, you might want to look into some solutions available that can get you out of harms way. If you are paying mortgage you might want to opt out by selling your home or else searching the marketplace for loans to help you refinance and get lower rates.

When you owe money, your debts are sent to collection agencies. Once you have a list of bad debts it leaves you open to court. Creditors are people you owe and if they send your debts to collection agencies, you might be waddling in quicksand since someone else has control of your life. If you are delinquent on payments creditors, can garnish wages from your paychecks, take hold of all your tax refunds, and send you to court. The only advantages you have when you have debts are the creditors cannot charge outrageous late fees or interest rates.

The creditors cannot take a post-dated check from you and cash it until they notify you first. Creditors cannot cash a postdated check ahead of its date. Creditors cannot ask for postdated checks by frightening you with criminal suits. Creditors are not permitted to send post cards in an effort to ask for payment, nor can creditors label, or place symbols outside of an envelope to press for payments.

There are many areas of legalities and illegal acts to look for if you are in debt and threatened with lawsuits, liens, repossessions, foreclosures, and judgments. Some of the most important areas of illegal acts made by collection agencies include false unlawful authorization forms, or sending out a representative of the collection agency posing as an officer of the law. Some creditors even harshly threaten debtors by using profanity or harassing family members by imitating government representatives.

Creditors have even tried cashing postdated checks and attempting to charge late fees for insufficient funds. It is important that you learn your rights when your credit is in jeopardy. If you are taking to court and know your rights, you might see a way out of a bad situation. If you know your rights you might even find a way to avoid court by taking another route to stall payments.

Some collection agencies have even threaten debtors by phoning their home at late hours of the night, calling friends, family and neighbors, and so on. If you suspect you are heading down bad credit path, then it is important to document all communications between collection agencies, lenders, and other sources so that you are prepared when or if you hit the courtroom. If you see that you cannot avoid court then you want to take all the necessary steps to cover yourself when you arrive on the door that is taking your control out of your hands.

It is important to know that you can trust only you in most cases. When your faith is in someone else's control the worst possible situation can happen. In most cases, however, there is always a solution to the problem and you have the right to stand up and take back some of your control.

Collection Agency

Credit repair and collection agencies go hand in hand since one is out to get the other. In other words, we sometimes run from our debts taking advantage of a kind gesture.

Collection agencies are not as kind as the lenders so therefore be warning...the collection agencies are on the loose.

We must understand how collection agencies work in order to find a way to stop hassling phone calls and letters. Collection agencies are a third-party source hired by creditors after the creditor has made every attempt to collect a debt without success. Collection agencies will search high and low and often play nasty little tricks trying to hunt you down. If you changed your address and typed your credit card into an online database, do not be surprise when the debt you tried to outrun catches up with you. Collection agencies tap into all types of resources in an effort to hunt down debtors. Collection personnel searches through phone directories, databases online, makes phone calls posing as a friend to luring the debtor in, sifts through the records at the post office, and so on.

There is no stone unturned when it comes to collection agencies in a search to find a debtor. The upside is many of the collection agencies make mistakes by hiring low waged servants to handle the job of finding debtors. When they are sifting through the files, they often loose contact since they have millions of records each day.

Now if a collection agency has affiliation with the three big bureaus then they have access to information that independent collection agencies do not have. If you are in a financial bind that makes it difficult to repay your debts, you will need to consider loosing yourself and leaving no traces when you leave. If you move do not freely hand your information, including address, phone, city, or other information to anyone you do not trust.

When you set up a phone account make sure that you have your phone unlisted. Do not apply for loans, credit cards, or anything that requires information from you. It is important to keep a low profile in your new area to avoid complications. This is the ultimate solution if find no other solution for getting out of debt. Problem!

The problem with running away from your debts is that in time it will catch up with you no matter how cautious you are. If there is no other way out then sometimes, we have to take a leave of absence, but if there is a solution, we need to search all options available to us first. One solution is negotiation. If you are hassled by creditors, it is time to send a letter recognizing your situation and asking for an extension on payments. If you make regularly payments working the debt down then you are on the right road to credit repair. If you debt has reached the collection agency you might want to call your creditor and ask them to take back your debts.

This means you will set up a plan to repay the charge against you and continue paying until that debt is paid in full. In return, your creditors will contact the collection agencies and let them know the debt is in current resolve.

Do not miss a payment when the creditors take back your debt. This will only frustrate the creditors since they were free to give you a second chance. If you call your creditors and ask for a take back on your debt and the creditor denies you but gives, you the opportunity to contact the collection agency to set up payment plans...by all means do it! If you are lucky enough to hear this from a creditor and the creditor as promises takes back your debt after you paid off the collection agency, you are taking steps to rebuilding your credit.

When you are in debt creditors will contact you first for up to four weeks in an attempt to collect. When you fail to make payments, the creditors contact the collection agencies who then pursue the debt. To avoid collection agency hassles deal with the creditors.

Where to Get Credit Resources?

If you are having problems with credit you might want to surf the market for resources that can help you find a way out of debt. The many resources available do not include the many spammers that tell you in three minutes we can get you out of debt. The scores of resources that offer a quick solution to repairing debt are only out to add more debt to your credit files. In reality, the only resource that can get you out of debt is yourself.

The solution then I am offering to you is the many guides, laws, and sources that are available to help you within adding more debt to your credit files. There are kits available that can lead you in the right direction to eliminating debt; however, some of the kits offered abroad the Internet are expensive. You can get the same kits in most cases at your local library or else other resources that offer debt repair kits abroad the Internet.

It is up to you to research the marketplace carefully to find the best prices, but ultimately you would want to start at the library. Two of the best guides available at many libraries are the DO-IT-YOURSELF KITS and the Solve your Money Troubles. Credit Repair Sixth Edition written by Attorney's Robin Leonard & Deanne Loonin is another great resource tool for getting help with credit repair.

If you are searching for a way out of debt, it makes sense to know what your score is on your credit files. You can order copies of your credit reports by contacting TransUnion, Equifax and Experian. The addresses are available in phone books and over the Internet.

The three major credit bureaus are obligated to give you FREE copies of your report once each year, however if you are not eligible for a free report you can get copies free once you apply for a couple of loans, or even one loan for that matter. I advise against this because each time you apply for a loan or credit card it goes on your credit file. Other resources available to you are found over the Internet. There is information available to help you see your way out of your situation.

Resources are a source of information and contacts that help you get started to repairing your credit. If you are suffering as a result of low income and creditors calling you every day, then it is important that you do not give up hope.

By calculating your monthly bills and setting up a budget that meets your requirements is a great resource for eliminating debts. It is also possible to earn money while you are broke. Cutting back on items, groceries, household goods, clothing, and other items can help you increase your income. You could also make money by selling valuable assets that are sitting in the corner of your home taking up space. If you cut back on utilities and entertainment, you might also find an increase in your pocket each month. Again, there are scores of resources available to you that can help you repair your credit.

Do it yourself Credit Repair

Many of us believe that it is only through an agency that we could possibly have any hope for repairing our own credit. Rest assured that this is not true. It could possibly cost you more money and time to arrange through an agency than it would to just do it yourself. My recommendation, before contacting an agency for assistance is to follow the steps below as you may just be surprised at the results.

Repairing your own credit takes time, and definitely takes patience. You first need to contact the credit reporting agencies in writing requesting your credit report. You are entitled by Federal Law to a free credit report every year. There are three main credit-reporting agencies that you will need to contact. The bureaus information can be located by running a search on the internet for "Credit Reporting Agencies" or looking through you local phone book. Include the following in your written correspondence with the credit agency.

1. Written request for a copy of your credit report (You are entitled to one free credit report a year).
2. Include a copy of your state ID.
3. Send proof of your current address if it is not current on your ID.
4. List your last known addresses for the past 5 years.
5. Include a copy of your social security card.
6. Sign the document

Allow at least 4-6 weeks to receive your credit report(s). If you have already received an annual credit report from an agency and are not entitled to the free yearly report, you may also use any denial letter of credit within 60 days of its receipt. If you receive a letter denying you credit, make a copy and enclose it with your written request for a copy of your credit report.

Once you receive your reports from all of the agencies, review each report for accuracy and differences. Design a spreadsheet or written log to track the differences. Do not hesitate to make use of disputes or accounts that are invalid. If you find anything on your report that is worth disputing, most agencies allow you to file an official dispute via their website.

Your credit reports should include contact and account information for each creditor. Organize all of your debt and creditors. Most debts older than 7 years old will or may not appear on your report, if this is the case, leave them alone, do not dig around for them. Most creditors after 7 years of not having any contact with you will write off the debt, some may continue their pursuit to locate you, either way, don't open the Pandora's box if the account isn't listed on your credit report.

Take it upon yourself to contact each creditor to make payment arrangements, most are willing to work with you, some may make your task very difficult. If a creditor is being difficult, feel free to ask for his or her supervisor or speak with someone else. Expect some creditors to be rude and unwilling to work with you, do not feel discouraged, and just ask to speak with someone else. Offer a settlement amount. Write down details of the conversation as well as the person's contact information every time you speak with a creditor.

It may take up to 6 months to feel like you are making any progress at all on your credit with your payment arrangements but rest assured that your credit will fall into place within a year.

It is very important that while you are paying your creditors, when you mail in your payment, that you pay by check or money order and keep all of your receipts. Always include a SASE (self-addresses stamped envelope) with your payment and request a receipt for the payment from the creditor.

Obtain copies of your credit reports on a yearly basis from each agency. Do not obligate yourself to any other creditors while paying off your current ones. You will or may receive several credit offers, throw them away. Stay focused on your goal to get out of debt and keep track of all your activity such as payments, contact with the creditors, their names, extension, time and date you spoke with them and list any details of your conversations and arrangements.

Defaults

If you have defaults on your credit record, it is possible to have some of them removed. Defaults are non-payments recorded on your credit files. When a person is in default, they are subjected to lawsuits, liens, judgments, and other complicated situations. If you are a student struggling to pay student loans, a renter struggling to meet monthly bills, or a homeowner battling to stay out of debt you might want to know what is available to you.

If you have a college loan, which means you have a loan from the government you can ask for a default, which gives, you time to repay the loan. Other types of defaults include insurance policies, bills, car loans, personal loans, and other types of credit lines.

Sometimes we are subject to debts that may not be ours. There are thousands of collection agencies and credit reporting services throughout the US. Sometimes there are errors sent to the credit bureaus that put the default on your credit file. Once the default goes on your credit file it remains there until the bill is paid in full. Now, if you did not make the purchase the first thing you want to do is file a dispute.

The problem however, defaults remain on your credit file for a period of time before they are removed. The upside is fighting for your rights and disputing the allegations made against you are telling creditors that some boo-booed. If either you have credit cards and purchased an item or service on the card and the service or item was defeated, you must first dispute the problem with the providers.

After you have disputed the issues with the providers, you will next contact your credit card lender and inform them of the defaults on your credit report. DO NOT pay on items or services that done you wrong, since this means the creditors will view you in a different light.

If you have, insurance policies are delinquent on your bills, you might lose your coverage, however in some cases you might be in more trouble than you realize. Read all terms & agreements as well as any other fine prints before obligating yourself to a contract. If there is a default against you on your policy contact your provider immediately and try to work out a plan.

By making contact, you could save your insurance as well as additional debts added to your accounts. Anyone that lends you a line of creditor subjects you to defaults if you cannot make payments. If you have defaults on your credit files make sure that you work to pay the debts down to avoid complications.

Identity Theft Victims

Identity theft victims are those people that loose simply because someone has stolen their identity and run up their bills. If you are victim of Identity Theft you are well-aware how difficult it can be to get back on your feet again. Identity Theft victims often have to go through a series of steps to repair their credit and identity.

Once the victim has made contact with the 3 credit bureaus they often put a Freud Alert on your credit report, which is supposed to be a protection to you, but the truth is it is a 'mistake' since it labels the victim. If you go to apply for a loan or credit card it is likely you will receive a rejection in the mail.

So, is there a solution for Identity Theft victims and how can they repair the credit? First, it is important to avoid Identity Theft by protecting your Social Security Card, Driver License and other important information about yourself. However, if you are already in the credit bureaus labeled under the Freud Alert, then you may find yourself giving up. Identities are stolen in several ways.

The Internet is swarming with predators waiting to mess up someone else's life. People may stand over your shoulder peeking down at you while you are keying in your PIN number at the bank. You might have been in a relationship and the person decides he/she owns you and when you break up that person takes your identity. There are several ways that your Identity can be stolen.

The solution is then protecting your identity with shields that no one can break through. If you are a victim of Identity Theft then your identity needs to be protected more so than ever. This sounds crazy since someone already has your ID. You will need to stay alert to the activities that affect your credit report. It is important that you keep updated copies of your reports at all time. If you notice activity, immediately dispute the claims against you.

Be sure to file a police report since you will need these reports to show the 3 bureaus and others that your identity has been stolen. Once you receive the reports make sure you send copies to each credit bureau so that the companies can get you on record. The companies are going to put up a Freud Alert once the copies are evaluated. Here is where you need to stay alert. Instead of Freud Alerts, the companies can put up a FREEZE on your accounts.

A Freeze gives you the options that Freud Alerts will not. For example, if you go to a bank and apply for a loan with a Freud Alert on your accounts, most likely you will be turned down. However, if the banks see that you have a FREEZE on your accounts, they will investigate and possibly give you the loan. Freeze means that someone has affected your life by stealing your identity, while Freud means that someone has committed a criminal act on your account, and that someone could very well be you.

You will also need to report any checks that you suspect were stolen. Monitor your banking account at all times to make sure that no out of place activities are going on. It is important that you alert your utility providers and anyone that you have open accounts with. If you have credit cards report them immediately to get replacements. You may even want to cancel your current bank account and open a new account.

This will offer a source of protection. It is also important that you contact your Social Security Office to find out if your Social Security has been used out of place. If actions have been listed on your card, be sure to let the Social Security Administrators know. Making others aware of what is going on in your life, can spare you additional headaches. You are already a victim of criminal behaviors, why not take the steps to repair your credit and restore your life. Finally, you will need to contact Washington D.C. or the Identity Theft Clearinghouse, Federal Trade Commissions and let them know you are a victim of Identity Theft.

Skipping to Build Credit

There are always solutions when it comes to repairing your credit. We sometimes go through problems in life that makes our life hard to manage. Sometimes we simply have to skip ahead in order to get ahead. If you have late bills and see that you can't meet these expectations be sure to make contact with your creditors letting them know your situation. If you have a situation that has put you out of work due to disability, you can let the creditor know that you will have a pension or other type of allowance coming soon.

This will stall your creditors and when you get the money you can put forth the effort to repairing your credit. If you are renting and have showed good payments in the past with your landlord you might ask him/her if they can wait a bit longer on payment so you can get caught up. If you are trying to save money to repair your credit, you might even want to look for a cheaper home to lower your costs.

On the other hand, if you own your home, you might want to look into some different options. If you see that your payments are going to be late in the next few months, it is always wise to contact your bank lender. If you made good payments in the past, lenders are often happy to waive late fees, unless it is interest only mortgages. If you appear to have a long-term financial situation your lender may offer a refinance option to help reduce your monthly mortgage payments. If the lender is not willing to help you find a solution you might want to check out other banks. Remember there is always an option. If you run out of revenues you might even consider selling your home. The solution is always best since many people are searching for homes that are repossessed or in foreclosure, or nearing one or the other.

Another option is giving the lender the keys and walking away from your obligation. This is an option if you owe more for the home than what it is worth. There are some disadvantages and advantages to any option you choose. The best solution is to estimate your monthly take home pay, and find a solution to making ends meet. When you take out a mortgage a wise man will often calculate all aspects before signing an agreement. Often, many homeowners take out a loan however and neglect to factor in long-term financial situations.

This is when it often fails and credit repair goes in motion. For the most part, refinancing or else asking your creditors for an extension is often better than walking away from your debt. Some debtors often hire a lawyer that tells them we can help. The fact is those lawyers will charge you more than you probably owe to help get the creditors off your back. Once your debts are paid, you might need another lawyer to get the first lawyer off your back.

Taking the smartest path to repairing credit is always wise. If you see that you are overwhelmed with debt you might even want to consider

Bankruptcy. Chapter 7 Bankruptcy is often a better solution than Chapter 13. Chapter 7 will free you from your debts permanently, with the exceptions of any current bills. The problem is when you file Bankruptcy, whether it is 7 or 13 it goes on your credit and you have another problem. In one way you repaired your credit, but by no means are you on the road to building your credit history.

Yes, it is true you can often get another car or home with a bankruptcy against you, but, I know that you will be searching high and low before you find the companies that will give you a loan. Bankruptcy stays on your record for ten years. So as you see, sometimes we have to skip ahead to get ahead. Skipping one bill to pay a more in demand bill is not necessary a bad thing. It takes a couple of months before your bills go to the 3 bureaus.

Chapter 5 - Credit Repair System

The Credit Repair System has tools available that helps many debtors find relief. Credit repair system is the steps to recovering from debts, while getting back on your feet again. If you have bad credit, you already know how difficult it is to reestablish a respect in society.

Struggling down many roads, I know you have asked over in your mind, "How can I get out of debt?" The truth is we all have had bad times and some of are able to get back on our feet again quicker than others do. Therefore, you are not alone in this fight to reestablish credit.

Even rich people have filed bankruptcy, so do not think you are centered out from the rest of the world. In this article, I am going to make it quick and to the point, helping you get out of debt through the process.

Repair System Kit:

I will guide you through a process that will lead you step-by-step through credit repair.

1. Get copies of your credit report from TransUnion, Equifax, and Experian.
2. Overview your credit report watching closely for errors (bills you did not accumulate)
3. Dispute any errors on your credit report immediately with the three credit bureaus
4. Once your report is clear start saving money, but cutting back, increasing your income, and continues disputing other debts that may occur if necessary.
5. Lay out a budget that matches your monthly installments, a separate budget that comes close to your debts as possible, and finally a budget that meets your demands on survival after you have cut back funds.
6. Finally, start paying on your secured loans first, and work through your unsecured loans gradually.

If you follow these steps to the letter, you will eventually see where it pays off. Starting with:

Step 1: we can see we need to know where we are out before we can get out of our situation. Having a basic overview of your report regularly can prevent your credit scores and ratings from being affected by errors or identity theft.

Step 2: is a basic outline of where you are at, where you are going, and how you will get there.

Step 3: is obvious. If you find errors on your report, the first thing you want to do before paying your debts is to clear up the wrong that has been done to you.

Step 4: is also obviously, since you want to find a solution to repairing your credit. If you save money by cutting back, finding a way to make more money, and budget you will have a guaranteed strategy to getting out of debt.

Step 5: the budges should match your financial situation allowing you to repay your debts and survive in the process. The budgets if carefully developed will allow you additional funds for savings if you plan your strategy right.

Step 6: once you start paying off your credit you will notice almost immediately a result. The result may be a rise in your self-esteem and confidence, but it is a start to a better future.

There is nothing more rewarding than being free of financial obligations. When you walk out in the public your friends, family and neighbors will acknowledge a nature high, and ponder on how they too can be like you. If you follow the steps you will not only notice results of relief, you will also notice an increase in your income.

In addition, if you have any debts that have not hit the collection agencies, find a solution for getting those bills up to date. You can call your creditors in the first four weeks of late bills and let them know your situation, including your financial status to repay the debt. Often creditors will make arrangements for you to pay each month on your bills.

Make sure you meet your creditors' expectations, since they took a chance on you in first place. This is the ultimate credit repair system that will get you out of debt. Debt Repair Agencies, Debt Consolidation, and other sources are often out to take advantage of the vulnerable, so relying on your self to get out of debt is the only system guaranteed to work most times.

Cut Back Credit Repair Solution

If you want to get out of debt, you need to cut back and start saving money. If you think you are going to get out of debt going on spending binges then you had better think again. Too many debtors believe once they are in debt it does not matter anyway so why not get what you want out of life.

The fact is you are taking advantage of yourself in the process of taking advantage of others. If you do not have the money and scraping for every penny you can get your hands on, this is one thing, but if you have extra cash and your bills are due, what are you doing? If you do not have the money to pay your bills then you are probably a low-income census. This means that you are eligible for commodities, income, items, and so much more.

You might want to start with your local Social Services and apply for Food Stamps, commodities, and income, including medical coverage until you get back on your feet again. Do not go in the door believing this is your way through life, since Welfare is only a temporarily resource available to the low-income families. If you found yourself in a predicament and can't see a way out you might want to seek advice.

Find someone that you can trust to guide you through the process of credit repair, otherwise you might want to ask someone with a Debt Counselor qualified to assist you. Any Religious Organization or at least most Organizations that Specialize in debt management or credit repair are the best sources to consult with. If you can find a way to cut back on your situation all the better, since most businesses, companies, individuals, and so on will tell you "oh we know a way," do not go for that, go for you!

You got in the debt; it will take you to get out. When it comes to relying on others to help you out, you might as well hang up the phone because no one is at home. Life is too short to go through the remaining revolution without a hint of confidence. When you feel that confidence building inside your next step should be obvious.

When you think no one cares, pick up the phone and dial yourself. You do care, and the fact is you care more than the creditors or collection agencies that are bugging you every day to pay or try to pay your debts. You are the source to getting out of your situation. Credit is an obstacle and if you want to run you are about to get yourself into a situation that you do not really need.

However, if you want to take the time and learn, earn, and ACCEPT, then you are on the road to recovery. If you are in debt over your head, do not run, rather stand up and fight for whom you are. Now that we are on the road to credit repair I want to let, you know that the Internet and many other resources are confusion.

Therefore, if you are in a <u>Chapter 7 Bankruptcy</u> obligated each month to pay more than you make...YOU do have the option of FILING Bankruptcy 13. DO not let anyone misled you! The fact is if you are paying more than you can afford to bankruptcy seven courts, you can get a bankruptcy 13 in motion. Chapter 7 means you have to repay your creditors while Chapter 13 means all your debts are wiped out. Notice...You will have a Chapter 13 on your credit report, but it does not mean that you cannot get credit.

In October, the laws are changing so if you are in a position where you see no other resolve, now is the time to get out. The economy, society and government make it difficult for all of us, so why not find a resolve when you can. If you do not see bankruptcy in focus find a way to cut back on your bills, groceries, home necessities, toiletry, insurance, and personal needs, and so on.

Debt Counseling Solutions

Is debt counseling a solution for credit repair?

Debt Counseling Services and Credit Services are Organizations that are sponsored by most of the creditors. Most Debt Counseling services are nonprofit organizations; however there is few that are on their own. Before you can contact a Debt Counselor you must have some source of income. The counselor provided you will often contact your creditors and alert them that you are making the effort to repay your debts. Once the creditors have been contacted, the organization will next work out an agreement that works with your current budget. After a decision has been reached you are expected each month to make a payment toward paying off your creditors. Your money goes first the organization where you have asked for help, and then is forwarded to your creditors.

Once the creditors receive your money, the Counselors ask the creditors to deduct a small amount of funds to pay for their services. There are some debt counselors that will waive interest on your balance, however, most counselors will not. If you are unable to meet your payments each month you might be required to pay late fees. The only real advantage you have by using a Debt Counseling Agency is that you won't see bankruptcy on your credit report although the two are similar.

The best solution then for repairing your credit is taking the ball in your own hands. If you take back the control that was robbed of you, you have the advantage of getting out of debt without further complicating your situation. One way of taking back your control is to set up a monthly budget plan that works to payoff your debts and leave you enough funds to survive. Survival takes less than most people believe in the sense we often purchase items we don't really need. If we purchase minimal grocery necessities and other necessities we will find more funds available.

There are several solutions for cutting back on house items for cleaning. Generally, soap and water is sufficient for cleaning your home. Better yet, if you have laundry detergent you can clean carpets, wash windows, clothes and so on. One solution is possible to handle multiple tasks; therefore buying multiple products for house cleaning is often a waste of money. The advertisements that tell you this product works better than the other is often a gimmick to lower you into a debt.

Another idea is it is possible to cook dinners that last for more than one day. Also, you could pack a lunch instead of buying out when you are at work or on a trip. If you are taking trips regularly and it isn't for business purposes, you might ask yourself how you can cut back.

When you cut back on trips you are cutting back on gas mileage, meals, and hotels and so on. Anytime you can find a solution to cut back you is making effort to repair your credit as long as you are spending the savings on your bills. If you are trying to save money for trips or items for your home, you might want to put this off until you get your bills paid.

Remember when you pay off your bills first, money will flow more freely for other desires in life. If you are having difficulties meeting monthly obligations contact your creditors and explain your situation. Many creditors will work to find a solution rather than taking a complete loss.

Be ware that some creditors are greedy and don't really care how hard times are for you. These types of creditors want money and they want it now! The best solution then for dealing with creditors is to payoff the most imperative bill first and work your way through each bill. If you have bills that are not necessary terminate them for a short-time until your credit is repaired. Bills such as cable or satellite, Internet if not used for work and other entertainments can wait. Bills are a part of our daily lives and avoiding bills is not a solution for repairing credit. Therefore, Debt Counseling is not the best solution for eliminating debt.

Chapter 6 - Establishing Credit, the Great Task

"How do I establish credit, when I do not have a credit history"?
This is probably the most commonly asked question by most consumers looking to open a credit account. Not having credit can be just as difficult as having bad credit unless you know how to go about proving yourself to a potential creditor.

The crazy catch twenty-two:

How can you get credit if nobody is willing to extend you credit because you don't have any credit history?

A good place to start is by obtaining a letter of credit from a company that you have been dealing with already that does not report to the credit reporting agencies.

An example would be your electric company. It is possible to contact your electric company and request a letter of credit. They are likely to require that you have had an account with them for at least a year as with most companies that you are asking for a letter of credit. Your cable company may be another option for a letter of recommendation for credit. If you have had an open account for at least a year and have made on time monthly full payments, without payment arrangements, these two companies are good candidates to provide you with a letter of recommendation for credit.

To establish credit either with or without a letter of recommendation for credit, you could also start with your banking institution. All banks offer credit card and loan accounts. If you have banked with the institution for at least a year (sometimes 6 months) they may strongly consider extending you a line of credit.

In the beginning of any credit account, your interest rate may be high, but don't despair, after your first positive review in about 6 months, the interest rate may fall dramatically as well as your payments if you have been making minimum payments.

Just to get you started. Your new account may be very low. After about

6 months of on time payments, your lender may review your account for a larger credit line. The smartest technique is to start with baby steps. Start with just a small account, pay the accounts regularly, get used to the monthly obligation, and make on time monthly payments before jumping into any other credit account(s).

You are very likely going to find creditors coming out of the wood work and hunting you down to offer you a line of credit, consider their offers with caution. Actually, the best recommendation is to give your self at least 6 months to a year before taking on a new account. Jumping in too fast can easily wipe out all of the hard work you have done so far to establish some credit.

Once you jump on the credit bandwagon, it is vital that you keep track of your own credit rating. You will find many great offers online for programs that can inform you, on a regular basis, of your credit standings. You could also request your free annual credit report and verify your status regularly.

Once your credit becomes active, keeping track of your credit report is crucial for many reasons:

1. It could prevent the use of a fraudulent credit account by an unknown user.
2. It could prevent the unfortunate event of somebody stealing your identity and using your credit.
3. It could help find a lost payment and assist you with keeping track of how your creditor is reporting your payment activity.
4. It is just good credit etiquette to know your own credit rating.
5. Knowing your own credit rating and status gives you bartering power when dealing with a new potential creditor.

Once you've established some credit, take caution with accepting credit offers from other creditors, look into the interest rate the lenders are offering, consider the monthly obligation in addition to your other financial responsibilities such as rent, utility bills, car insurance, groceries, laundry expenses, gas, day care, etc., and feel free to decline credit offers.

In the beginning of your adventure with new credit accounts, it can be very exciting to have several creditors offering advances, it can be an uplifting and powerful event, however, pursue with caution in order to maintain a healthy credit rating and score. Keep your credit history in mind and respect the great task that you have accomplished by establishing credit with caution.

Government Credit Repairs

If you are building a credit history, suffering bad credit or else your credit is great, there are sources available that will help you maintain credit, repair credit, and build credit history. If you have bad credit you must at least apply for two loans and be turned down before, the government will consider giving you a loan. Your credit report is not what is important, rather declines is the focus.

There are government loans available that help people start a new business, loans for single parents, loans for education and so on. The government offers loans to the special individuals and often has 0% interest or low interest against the loans. The government also offers grants to assist people in getting back on their feet again and the grants are yours. You do not have to repay the government anything, but you must use the money for what it was applied for.

DC recently reported that there are new sources available that makes it easy for families and individuals to repair their credit and get back on their feet again. When credit is bad, we have difficulty when applying for a home, car, apartment, credit cards and so on. We are virtually disregarded in most all cases. Today private lenders and the government are teaming up to make our economy more productive by helping those in need, including repairing credit.

Other resources are available helping those of us that are re-entering the employment market as well as helping those of us without jobs. There are funds available to those of us with low and high-risk credit scores. If you need a home, consolidate debts, car, or else start up your own business the government and private agencies are waiting to help you along. Reduced loans and free programs are available that will benefit millions in the economy that are suffer with bad credit histories.

Legal Aid is one source available that can help you with repair of your credit, as well as many other sources and this source is free of charge in most all cases. If you are paying, high fees to rent an apartment you might want to fill out an application with HUD. HUD pays a certain amount toward your monthly rent each month and you are required to pay the remaining balance.

Think of the money you will have left each month to apply toward building your credit history. HUD also has a solution for first time homebuyers with bad credit. Under the Homebuyers Bill of Rights allows us the right to purchase a home if we have bad credit. The government resources and private institutes has lowered their Interest Rates to around 5% to homebuyers and extends up to $500,000 for first time buyers helping them buy a home. The government and private institutes are also offering debt consolidation loans assistance with late payments, people that are starting a new business, and home improvements. Imagine the potentials?

It is often difficult for us when our credit is bad and not knowing where to start to repair our lives is even more frustrating. If you are suffering bad credit, you might want to check in to a few options available to you that can help you get out of debt. Life does not have to be difficult and all of us make mistakes.

The Fair Credit Reporting Act (FCRA) offers us protection on our credit report. Our privacy, fairness, accuracy and other laws says that we do have hope. If you are searching for a way to get out of debt you might want to start up your own business. The government has programs specifically for small business owners.

The programs will help business owners to finance their business and guarantees loans to those that are creating a plan to support them as well as paying their taxes to the government. This is a wonderful solution for getting back on your feet again and getting those creditors off your back. To find out more about small business loans check with your local bank. Bad credit is misery, but it does not have to be a force that destroys your life forever.

Student Credit Repair Solutions for Building Credit

There are solutions for students to repair their credit. Believe it or not but it is possible to get out of a student loan obligation. First you must determine what type of student loan you owe. Once you come to this determination you will next need to contact the proper sources and ask them to terminate your loan. If you can't repay the student loan this is the best option, since you are at risk of a law suit, garnishing of wages, or loss of tax refunds.

It depends on the time when you took out the loan and what type of loan you are under obligation to repay, but for the most part you can call and ask for a cancellation. If your school is negligence and has issued you a loan under false pretense, you may be able to cancel your loan. Also, if you are disable and see that you can no longer work, you may be eligible for a cancel of payment. If you are in the military, of a full-time member in certain organizations you may be able to cancel your loans.

Also, if you have paid your loans fatefully yet it comes a time you are having difficulty making ends meet, you may qualify for a deferment on your payments. Your lenders may even offer you an option of 'forbearance' if they decide they don't want to defer your payments. This means they will temporarily lower your monthly student loans until you are able to meet regular payments.

There are many options available to students in a rut. If you have sought out all options and nothing has proved results you may want to consider a consolidation loan. Usually when you ask for a loan consolidation your payments are lower each month. The downside with consolidating loans is that some of the companies that offer this option will charge monthly fees and interest against your loan.

This means you will be paying minimal payments on your combined loans, putting you at risk, while paying a fee to the consolidator. You might want to consider refinancing your student loans. This is an option available to you. Some banks will offer you a loan so that you can repay your current loans. This gives you the advantage of paying off one debt and lowering your monthly installments on other debts. You might even want to look at asking for grants that help pay your student loans. Sometimes we are able to apply for a FASA grant that we don't have to pay back.

This option means that the government will payoff some or all of your student loan. Rarely does the government payoff loans unless the student has high potentials of achieving. You could also ask for a flex payment on your student loans. If you have a Stanford Loan you have the course of ten years to repay this loan back once you graduate. The flex loan is an option where you call and ask for an extension on your loan. This gives you more time to repay the loan and hopefully your school efforts would have paid off by then. It is possible to repay a student loan in the course of 30 years, if you know what you are doing.

This means that you will pay higher payments each month over a period of time, and as time progresses you can pay lower monthly installments. The problem with these types of extensions on loans is that you are not repairing or building your credit, rather you are digging a deeper hole to bury yourself.

The reason is interest is attached to this type of offer and often those interest rates add up to thousands of dollars. Before you get into any obligation make sure you know what you are getting into. If you can get the government to pay off your student loans, obviously this is the best option for repairing credit. Student loans are an obligation that sometimes leads to a headache. Remember when you applied for a loan you took an oath to repay a debt that could benefit your future. Therefore, finding a solution is the best recourse to repairing credit.

Keeping Track to Repair and Build Credit

Keeping track of your spending and diverting a budget plan is often a better solution for repairing credit and building your rating. If you file for bankruptcy of debt consolidation you are only adding more headaches to an already bad situation. Bankruptcy goes on your credit report for more than ten years in most cases. When lenders see that you have filed bankruptcy they often stop you at the door. Debt consolidation loans add additional expenses to your bills.

Most debt consolidation loans include high interest rates, and payments to creditors that are insufficient and often keep you on needles and pins while your bills are paid. Therefore, the best solution for repairing your credit and building your rating is to save money. First, you might want to invest in software programs that have tools for budgeting and saving. The small investment could save you headaches by allowing you to use tools.

Keeping a record of your expenditures will start with a monthly budgeting scheme. If you are using software programs it is easier to budget, but if you choose to go on your own, you can set up a form. The form will have a header Daily Spending for the week of .... You will add in each day of the week, how much it cost you each day to survive, and the total of the week once the week has ended. It is wise to make several copies so that you can monitor your spending over the next few months.

Since Sunday is considered the first day of a starting week, it is always wise to start on a Sunday recording your budgets. Be sure that you record all of your spending, as well as money saved, earned, taxes, fees for banking, and so on. At each week when your bills are due try spending as much as possible on your bills, only allowing x amount of dollars to survive the following week. For example, if you have a phone bill of $113, a water bill of the amount $79, lights $89, gas $99 and you have the amount of $375 paid to you, you know that you can't pay the full amount of the bills to survive. Therefore, you will need to set up a budget to meet the demands put on you. It is wise to cut back. If you have cable or satellite TV, you might want to disconnect until you get your bills caught up.

You can always rent movies for a low fee each month online, or get a movie or two once every week for entertainment, however, if you can do without entertainment altogether until your bills are paid, how much better to repair your credit. Your credit is more important to your future than any single movie, unless you are making millions from the movie.

Radio music is often free, as well as other entertainments. Try to find something that doesn't cost until your bills are paid, then you can restore your life. You might even want to create a form that estimates your monthly installments as well as your expenses for survival. On the monthly form you will list your gross pay, bonuses, pensions, retirements, child support, and so on.

Finally, you will calculate your monthly receives and deduct them by the amount you owe, leaving enough funds available for your survival. While you are calculating your expenses make sure that you find ways to cut back on areas of your spending. This will help you to find a way to alter your spending habits, yet survive each month. After you have saved for a few months you will see that you have more money to spend toward your credit repair.

Cut backs should include groceries, personal care, medical, pet expenses, gifts, vacations, and so on. Keeping track of your records can help you to repair your credit rating and score as well as help you to rebuild your credit. If you have a low paying job you might want to find a job that pays better wages. You might even want to take a part-time job to compliment your full-time job. There is always a solution for building credit or else repairing what is already lost.

Knocking Down the Debts with Credit Repair

If you take a hard look at your situation and analyze your debts carefully, you might just find a solution to knocking down the debts. Debts are bills we owe to creditors, someone or source that has extended us a line of credit believing that we will pay the debt on time.

When creditors notice that you are behind on your bills they often wait a few weeks before notifying collection agencies and reporting you. In this length of time, you can write your creditors and ask for an extension or a reduction on your debt so that you can knock the debt down slowly.

Most creditors want the money and will extend your time to repay the debt, since they do not want to go through the hassle that comes along with reporting you. Most creditors want their clients to return and believe that if they give you a chance you will repay your debt and open a new account. If you do not contact your creditors and ask for an extension the creditors, want to remain the nice guys so they hand your over to the hounds.

Once the collection agencies receive your files, they begin their hunt and will go to all lengths to hunt you down, including breaking some laws to find you. Collection agencies often do not care whether you return to the creditors or not, rather they are paid a percentage for each debt collected. It is all about the money honey, so getting ahead is the best solution for repairing debt.

Collection agencies could care less if you have $1 to feed your kids, or else if you fall over from a heart attack as a result of them hassling at you. Collection agencies are in it for the money. Knocking down your debts upfront is a sure way of repairing your credit. After you have contacted each creditor, you can start setting up a budget plan that will help guide you through the process of eliminating your debts.

Start with a weekly budget plan and then work your way toward a monthly plan. Once you have a budget plan set up check the balance in each checking, saving or money marketing account regularly. If you do not have a savings, account open one. Make sure that the account does not have fees or interest rates attached.

If you have difficulty-managing money you may want to open a PayPal account and apply for a debit card online. This account not only protects you against identity theft, it also makes it difficult for you to get money right away. Put your debit card where you can't find but in a safe place. PayPal accounts often pay back money when you spend so if you want to pay your bill with the PayPal card you will get 1% of that spending returned to your account.

This is a solution, but you have to learn how to manage your money and yourself in order to repair your credit and get out of debt. When people feel out of control, it often affects their lives tremendously. Therefore, when you take control of your situation you are restoring human natures within. Putting a stop to collection agencies is a big step toward a brighter future. If you need help getting out of debt there are resources available to you. The many resources that do not include additional debts to your credit are the best solutions for repairing your credit.

You might want to even search for loopholes in the system to find a way out of debt. If you are low income and have bad credit there, are government loans and grants available. By searching the marketplace, you just might find out that you qualify for a loan or grant from the government.

There are also possibilities that include getting creditors to drop your credit completely. If you do not take the step to learn what is available to you, you will never get out of debt. So if you want to avoid the hounds stay on the porch with the dogs and knock those debts down!

Chapter 7- Options to Avoid in Credit Repair and Building

There are several options available that make people believe it is a solution for freeing themselves of debts. One solution you want to avoid is borrowing money from finance companies. The companies that advances for consolidating loans and requires that you put your home or car up for collateral are often a source for getting your in deeper debt.

Most of the companies are offering a secondary mortgage against your home, and often the interest rates out outrageous. Most of the companies offer secured loans, but few of them offer unsecured loans. This is not an option for repairing your credit.

Another option you want to avoid is taking out a tax refund loan. This solution will get you fast cash, but the fees for this type of loan are often high. If you are getting $800 back in tax refunds, you will probably only get around $700 or $725. Another type of loan you want to avoid is the payday loans. Payday loans are loans against your paycheck.

Payday loans require that you write a check for the amount of loan to repay as well as the amount that you will pay the lender for borrowing the money. Payday loans eventually cost more money than what you have in the first place, and is not a solution for repairing your credit.

Pawn Shops are also a bad area to start in building your credit. Most Pawn Shops will take your merchandise, pay you half in some cases of what it is worth, and give you a certain amount of time to purchase your merchandise back before they sell.

Often there are interest rates on the loans provided by the business. It is certainly a way to loose all your belongings and halt you from repairing your credit. We can also take a look at debt consolidation. Although debt consolidation is much better than bankruptcy, it is not a solution for repairing your credit. Most debt consolidation companies drain the restricting resources by charging fees for the service. Many of the debt consolidation companies will pay the creditors minimal balance and put your assets at risk.

Unfortunately most of the debt consolidation companies will charge high interest rates, or high monthly fees to use their services. The best solution then is if you have a few extra dollars call your creditors directly and see if you can get them to negotiate a monthly installment that meets your expectations. This will provide you the time you need to find a solution for getting extra cash to payoff your debts. In some instances you can negotiate with your creditors and they may offer a lower amount than you owe so that you can repay the bills.

The downside with getting creditors to accept a payoff for less than you owe, is that you may be paying the IRS more in taxes. If the creditor writes off what you owe, or else settle for a lesser amount than what you owe, it is often reported to the IRS. Of course it seems like a no win situation when it comes to repairing credit, and working to rebuild your credit rating, but in the long run the rewards are sitting waiting for your arrival. Anytime you make efforts to repay back what you owe another individual or company, is rewarding when your self-esteem, self-confidence and other essential human necessities are restored. None of us like to owe money to anyone, but some of us have no choices at times.

If you are not prepared to deal with your creditors on your own, you could consult with credit assistances that work to help individuals restore their credit. The United Way is one source that works with your creditors to help restore your credit. Creditors often prefer to negotiate with respected businesses rather than deal with individuals or lawyers.

Debt counselors and Nonprofit Organizations that work to repair credit for individuals will often help you to decide how much is owed and how much each month you can afford to repair your credit and build your credit rating. There is always a solution in credit repair, so never give up!

Requesting Payment Options to Repair Credit

When you are in debt the best solution for repairing your credit is to ask for extensions, or arrange payment plans. If you have student loans, you can call your loan officer and request deference on your payments. If you are turned down on deference, you can ask for forbearance. Forbearance is a postponement of your monthly installments. Most times, it is easier to get forbearance than deference.

The problem is your interest rates accrue even when no payments are made. The forbearance against your loan often lasts six months to two years and then you are expected to pick up regular payments. If you are suffering debt related problems then this is a great solution for getting out of debt. You can also consolidate your student loans. If you have been turned down for deference, forbearance your next solution is fill out an application for a loan to repay your debts. It is also possible to refinance your student's loans.

If your credit is severe, you might however have difficulty with getting support on consolidation. You also have the option of requesting a flex payment plan. If you have a FFELP Stafford Loan ask for an extension on your loan, or else ask for a renewal on your loan for payments that allow you to pay according to your current income. The downside is when you seek other people's help for resolving your debt issues you are only adding more debts to your plans.

Defaults

It is possible to get out of a default if you have made payments faithfully in the past, but can no longer repay your debts. First, you must apply for a plan that is 'reasonable and affordable.' The plan applies to your current financial situation and if you faithfully make six months of payments on time, you may qualify for a default. The default does not excuse you from the debt but allows you to make payments according to your financial situation.

If you obtain the default it is important to pay off your dues on times, since it is not possible to obtain a second default. If you faithfully pay toward your default for a year, you can slide through some loopholes and get the default dropped. The downside is when you apply for a default and makes your payments, in the long run your payments increase. This is a temporarily solution for debt relief.

Credit Repair Doctor Bills

If you have doctor, dental, or lawyer debts and need a solution, be aware there is an option available. If you owe a lawyer, doctor or dentist it is wise to contact them as soon as possible and negotiate. Most lawyers, doctors and dentist will work out a payment agreement lowering your monthly installments. Some reduce your bills, while others will completely wipe out interest charges or late fees.

Most times lawyers, doctors and dentist will put off sending your debt to a collection agency providing you meet your agreed payment each month on time. If you suspect you will be late sending payment, make sure you contact the creditor immediately to avoid complications. If you make contact with the creditors, it tells them that you are not trying to avoid your problem rather you are delayed.

It is essential to careful review your bills each month searching for errors and disputing them immediately if any occur. After your review your bills and there are no errors found find a resource for paying each bill immediately. This is the ultimate solution for repairing credit or saving your credit. If you have, credit cards make sure you meet monthly installments regularly to avoid paying additional rates per month.

Car Loans

Finally, if you have a car loan and see that you cannot meet monthly installments contact your creditor immediately. Be sure to tell your creditor your situation and ask for an extension or else a lower payment for the month. DO NOT lie to any creditor. Lying only complicates matters worse. If you lender sees that you can make next month's payment, or else repay your debt for the month at a later time they may excuse your tardiness. However, if the creditor sees this is a long-term financial issue they may refinance your vehicle providing you lower monthly installments and lower interest rates.

Laws in Credit Repair

There are certain laws issued for people that have bad credit and to know these laws is important to protect all those involved in your life. The Federal Legislation and several other agencies including the Fair Credit Reporting Act (FCRA) protect you from collection agencies and creditors. If you have bad credit you really want to read this article especially if you are being harassed by creditors or else threatened. First, we are going to look at what steps debtors can take to protect their status.

Debtors have the right to ask collection agencies or any source hassling them for debt collection to stop hassling them. You must contact the collection agencies immediately and request that they stop communication with your completely. It is important to word your letter wisely avoiding giving them ammunition against you. You can do this if your collection agency has claimed a lawsuit against you, or if the date has ended, where the creditors can no longer contact you.

If the collection agency has written several letters or made several phone calls threatening you with a lawsuit, you can write an informal letter asking the agencies to stop nagging you. If you have a current debt, it is wise to negotiate with the creditors, since some may reduce your balance or even dropped the debt completely. If the debt is older than seven years, it is important that you DO NOT communicate with a collection agency regarding the bill. At the seven-year period, the account should have been removed from your credit report. If it has not these people are in violation.

There are several reasons why creditors will disregard lawsuits. Some of those reasons include reductions in their chances of winning the suit. If your debt is old then collectors avoid paying high attorney fees to collect the balance. Therefore, knowing is glowing when you have bad credit. If you owe a debt, you have the legal right to protect your self against creditors. The best solution is stop ignoring the problem and finding a solution to repair your credit. Problems do not go away, rather they add up more problems. Credit repair is a deduction so you do not want to add on more than you can take.

Collection agencies under the law cannot correspond with you by sending mail to your address with symbols or labels. Collection agencies cannot call your mom and dad, or any family member regarding your debt. The collection agencies are obligated by law to cease communication if you have been subpoenaed to court.

Collection agencies are under law to avoid calling debtors after 9pm or before 8am. (Some laws state that the collection agencies cannot call after 10pm and before 5am.) If you have an attorney and the collection agencies know this and calls anyways, immediately file a complaint to the proper agencies regarding the action. It is important to document all information when you are in debt. This can protect you when the moment arises. If you have a job and a collection agency calls your work environment he or she is in violation of the law. (Note: If your employer allows calls, the law may not be effective)

Collection agencies are prohibited from impersonating law enforcement or government officials in an effort to collect a debt. At no time is a collection agency allowed to make available to the public information regarding your debts. Collection agencies are prohibited from sending letters, making phones calls, or acting out any form of communication that insinuates false impersonation.

It is also against the law for collection agencies to repeatedly call your home requesting you or threatening you to pay the debt. If a collection agency phones your home, they must comply by the law and identify their name and the companies name within one minute of the phone conversation. Finally, collection agencies are prohibited to list debtors on the 'deadbeat' list. Many laws and regulations apply to both collection agencies and debtors. Therefore, when you know the law you have strength to protect your self and a possible solution to avoid the law. If your credit is bad, the first step to a resolve is paying your dues and knowing the laws.

Information is this email is for information purposes only. Always contact your lawyer if you need legal advice.

Lawyers are not always a Good Solution

Lawyers often charge high fees to help individuals get out of debt. Credit repair clinics are available to assist individuals with debt relief, but only the absolute desperate would even consider these types of solutions. So, if this is not the solution for repairing credit, then what is? Many people that suffer from bad credit often wallow in a pond of self-pity believing there is no escape. Most people sit around waiting for the miracle that came to their neighbor's door to hit their door.

The fact is there are no miracles that happen unless someone takes the first step to eliminate the problem. We all suffer at times, and some of us more than others. It depends on the amount you owe, but for most of us getting out of debt is possible. Let's consider Bankruptcy Chapter 7. Chapter 7 Bankruptcy allows families and individuals to erase many of the debts owed to consumers. Chapter 7 Bankruptcy will often erase medical bills, home mortgage, car payments, and credit card bills.

The disadvantage with Chapter 7 Bankruptcy is that you will have to give up some of your assets in most instances. Once you fill out the appropriate papers you will then go into an 'automatic stay' which stops all your creditors from contacting you. This means that the creditors cannot garnish money from your checks each month to apply toward the bills you owe. It also means that the creditors cannot deduct money from your checking, savings, money market accounts and so on.

You are also protected temporarily since the consumers are not allowed to discontinue your electric or gas. The advantage of Chapter 7 Bankruptcy is that you have a degree of control over all assets and income that are available once the bankruptcy is in motion. There are debts that cannot be wiped out by filing Chapter 7 Bankruptcy. Those debts include child support payments, college tuition loans, criminal fines and costs, or other similar bills.

The problem with filing bankruptcy is that new laws are coming that will make it more difficult for debtors to file. The new laws in motion are nearly prohibiting debtors from finding a solution. Another form of bankruptcy that is available is the Chapter 13 Bankruptcy. Chapter 13 Bankruptcy means that the debtor keeps their assets while making lower monthly installments on their belongings.

This is a good solution for building credit. If you missed car or home payments it is a solution to help you repair your credit. The downside with Chapter 13 is that if you miss payments the courts has the right to change your plans. If the courts see that the delay is only temporarily they may issue you a 'grace period' until you get back on track, otherwise you might get a 'hardship discharge,' which means that your debts are dismissed.

The best solution then is finding a solution for the problem that won't lead you into the courtrooms. This is only a headache since you will have to make court meetings, be in someone else's control, and so on. The first step to repairing your credit and building to a better future is put some taps on your spending habits. Setting up a budget plan is a great start to credit repair without hitting the courts. Before long the law is going to make it virtually impossible for anyone to go to bankruptcy court, so it is time to get started now.

If you are not good at budgeting, there are Nonprofit Organizations that will help you set up a budget plan for little or no cost. Remember you are not alone, and there are people out there willing to help you get back on your feet. If you don't want to bother someone else with a budget plan you could also purchase software programs that offer the tools for budgeting. Quicken and many other software programs have excellent spreadsheet programs, analyzing tools, and so on to get you on the road to budget your money in order to repair your credit. Information is this email is for information purposes only. Always contact your lawyer if you need legal advice.

Chapter 8 - Solutions to Repairing and Building Credit

If you are in debt it might be wise to sell a few of your items to get the funds to repay your creditors. If you are selling your items to get out of debt you can think long-term and see that you can gradually replace your items once your debts are repaid. If you have a mortgage or car payment or both and can't afford to meet payments it would be in your best interest to sell.

This will not only help get you out of debt. Often when you resell your items you can make extra cash to repay your debts and possibly have funds left over. If you don't have items to sell you might want to look into several options available for repairing your credit and begin the process of building your credit score and ratings.

Of course if you are in debt you want to cut back on expenses in an effort to save money to get out of debt. Often we purchase items we don't really need. If you have a lot of items in your home you could also have a garage sale or yard sell. This is an excellent way to make a few extra dollars.

Another great solution is negotiating with your creditors. If you call each creditor and explain your situation, your creditors might offer you a monthly installment that can meet your expectations. Any solution or ideal is better than no movement at all. Finding a solution is not always as difficult as it seems.

Let's take a look at cutting back on expenses to get your starting on credit repair:

- What is the amount you pay each week on groceries?
- Do you use coupons to save?
- Do you purchase products or groceries on sale, or do you pay the high fees for name brands?

Finally, do you buy groceries in bulk, or do you go to the store regularly buying only a few items?

Ok, to build your credit you know you need money.

If you use coupons, or buy items on sale you are saving money and taking a step toward repairing your credit, since the savings can be applied to your credit bills.

- What about gas spent to travel?
- Do you go places that you don't really need to go?
- Do you spend more on gas simply because you haven't tuned up your vehicle?
- What about carpooling?
- Is it possible you could split gas bill with other individuals that work at your company?

Remember a penny saved is a penny earned.

- What about at home?
- Do you cut back on electricity, gas, and other utilities?
- Is it possible you can cut back and save some money toward your credit repair?

Ok, you might have cable or satellite.

- Is it possible you can do without this commodity until you get your bills caught up?
- What about subscriptions to books, magazines or music?

If you enjoying reading books or magazines the libraries often have the books and magazines that you would normally pay for through subscriptions.

- How about work?
- Do you eat out?
- Why not carry a bag lunch to work instead of eating out?

There are other areas we can cut back on. Areas such as buying second hand clothing, shopping at yard sales, spend less money on vacations and holiday gifts, and so on. Each time we cut back we will notice that our money is working toward a stable life. When we work toward stability we are on our way to repairing our credit ratings and score and working in the right direction toward repairing our lives.

Also, we could sell items on eBay to earn cash. Regardless of which solution is right for you, a solution is one-step in the right direction. If you are not sure which direction is right for you, you might want to consider investing a Credit Repair Kit. The price is generally around $30 more or less, but it can get you on the road to repairing credit. Remember one bill paid is one step out of debt. Finally, you will need to meet your bills requirements in order to get out of debt.

Reversing Credit Repair

If you want to reverse your credit repair and land deeper in debt, let me show you how. Have you ever seen the advertisings that say you qualify for $10,000 in credit and your credit will increase once you accept the terms & conditions and also send them some upfront fees?

How about the ads that say the Government will give you $25,000 in grant money and all you have to do is provide your personal information online and include an upfront to cover our costs?

Ok here is another reverse credit repair solution. If you see ads that say, you are guaranteed a credit card regardless of your credit history and you only pay $399 upfront in charges to secure your debts?

The list is only a few of the spammers that are out to put you in a jam. For instance, Trust Benefit offers credit cards and when you make the steep payment of $299 it won't take long before you realize that you put the gears in reverse and you are going down deeper in debt. There is no source on the marketplace that claims to restore your credit for a fee is ready to help you get out of debt.

The truth is if you want to move forward in repairing your credit you have to find a way to come up with the money to do so. You are responsible for your bills and if you are, suffering hard times the first step to repairing your credit is contacting your creditors and letting them know your situation. Often the creditors will work out a plan with you to help you repair your credit. If you are in debt, you might want to take on an extra job or else find a better paying job to make ends meet.

You might even want to sell some of your assets and pay off your debts. Material is irrelevant compared to your life and credit history. If you have bad credit, most people shun you when you ask for help. Even if you can only send $10 each week or month, it is a step forward to repairing your credit. You never want to go in reverse when your future is at stake. Credit is serious and if you are delinquent then many lenders will reject you once they review copies of your credit files. You might even apply for a job and are turned down if the company decides to take a look at your credit files.

Worse, you may find your self-homeless and when you apply for an apartment, the property owner may turn your away after reviewing your credit report. There are many negatives that can affect you when you have bad credit, so to move ahead you have to take the first step.

Do not waste your time searching for ads that claim to get you out of debt in a little time for a fee. Just because they claim to be Credit Repair Experts doesn't mean that they are qualified to get you out of debt. Credit repair is tricky, simply because there is a wealth of information available and many laws to abide. Therefore when you are repairing credit and do not know where to get started you may start at your local library.

The library has a wealth of information and often the right tools to get you started in repairing your credit. The library is not out to take you for a ride, so there is no better place to search. I am often skeptical about referring anyone to the Internet simply because too many predators are out there waiting to take advantage of the vulnerable. However, there is some great information aboard the World Wide Web; you just have to educate yourself before taking that route to repairing your credit.

To avoid reversing your credit repair process you have to learn and know what you are looking at before starting out on your adventure. Learning is the virtue of all humankind that makes it possible for man to move ahead. We can learn from our mistakes but if we are learning in reverse, we might as well toss in the towels.

WARNING About Credit Repair

The loans that are unsecured will be your duty, however for the most part your risks are far reduced. It's best for constructing your credit report if you're able to take good care of both secured and unsecured loans at precisely the exact same time. It's necessary that you keep alert to the warnings about the market by placing your own life into the hands of someone else, as you have more at stake.

Lenders who examine credit reports look in your credit history. They are going to consider you if your repayment history demonstrates that you had poor credit but you took the measures to pay off your money.

Scammers inform us that they can remove bankruptcies, create new identities, and eliminate dents in the credit report, and conclusions. That is what these firms are there scammers. The simple truth is that you and only you are able to make the proper moves. Yes, there's help available however, it requires patience, wisdom, effort, tools, wisdom, and investigating to get the resources. As soon as you find the tools they can help you escape debt. Before the time permits, your negatives and advantages will stay on your credit report. Steer clear of these kinds of organizations possible.

Credit repair is complex and catchy, but the truth is that there is not any resource available that may lift credit issues that are precise, or information from the credit reports. Unless it's insolvency, credit reports shop data and people can remain on your documents for 10 or even 15 decades. The Federal Trade Commission (FTC) recently set out reports alerting individuals with poor credit histories to prevent Credit Repair Clinics, along with other resources which promise to eliminate barriers in the credit reports. More than a dozen bureaus claim to fix charge in the procedure for promises.

There are before they help you however you need to pay upfront. As soon as you start clearing your charge and make contact the creditors will detect if you try to apply for another loan. It's very important to look after all loans that are secured because these kinds of loans put you in danger compared to loans that are unsecured.

If at all possible, take a loan with security attached to settle your debts and be certain to meet with the obligations in time. You could open accounts with department stores or gasoline stations to reestablish. There are methods however then you're headed in the wrong direction if you're relying on sources which fees to receive your from debt or promise to get you out of debt. It's crucial to avoid paying charges that Credit Repair Services charge if you're attempting to find a solution to fix your credit. It's crucial to dispute all claims who are false in your credit report. You also need to look after any reports on your credit report to prevent decreasing your credit. The entire world is swarming with predators. A few of the sources say that they could fix your credit in no more than three minutes, but others inform you no more than 25 days.

If your credit report indicates that you're currently fighting to make payments you will find a rejection notice. Bank creditors aren't required to send rejection letters, but they send them giving the chance to speak to the 3 credit agencies to you. For fixing credit the solution is currently taking control of your life and paying off these debts. It looks like a no win scenario, but the reality is every time you pay a bill it reduces your risks of judgments, lawsuits, liens, and credit. By paying back your accounts As soon as you clear your credit report you may see improvement immediately.

Conclusion

Finally, in order to start repairing your credit rating, you must begin a chronological sequence of actions that will require credit reporting bureau, creditors, debt collectors, and other things with which you engage in monetary transactions to ensure that the information that they collect, report, and /or market about you're precise. This info is in use to rely on your credit rating and when it is inappropriate, wrong, obsolete, or anything wrong on it may damage your credit score instantly and in addition to the credit score as years beyond its initial entry in your credit history. A different perspective of fixing your credit rating influences understanding credit and how many types of credit may assist or harm your credit ranking and credit rating. You need to evaluate your ability to capitalize on the various credit choices and take advantage of these credit forms which are going to be virtually advantageous for you at any given time or in any given condition. Life instances like graduation, employment, or marriage may influence your ability to get or sustain certain types of credit. For your credit and financial histories, as gathered and recorded by credit reporting bureau, may be responsible for improving or damaging your credit rating and credit score if you are not responsible for monitoring the information that's complied on you consider action to make sure that it's correct. You're probably aware of regular credit reports compiled around you which outline your financial history, but there are two types of credit reports that may be bought about you. A normal credit report is a report that many creditors and creditors buy. An investigative credit report may also be bought, which contains more comprehensive information regarding your financial history and your behaviors. As if which weren't enough, there are also other kinds of consumer reports which are used to profile your worthiness in different kinds of transactions that involve money. Insurance companies, companies, and other business entities buy consumer reports about you which include information other than credit histories. They also purchase scores which are apart from credit scores but relate to the specific area of interest. While these other customer reports and scores might not directly affect your credit score, they might be used to damage your capacity to engage in activities that you thought just your credit score would be used to qualify for. When there are lots of factors involved with repairing your credit score, your personal commitment to fixing your score is important. You, not the credit reporting bureaus, your creditors, nor the government will take

98

responsibility to repair your credit rating for you. This publication will provide you all the information that you'll need to begin repairing your credit

CONTACT ME
For more information and dispute letters that I use go to
NBACREDITREPAIR.COM
You can email me at
NBACreditRepair@gmail.com OR GetYours@BusinessCreditAsap

Building Business Credit
For information on business consulting and building business credit
to gain access to 50K in unsecured financing check out these
resources below:

OTHER RESOURCES

Business Consulting - SavvyBusiness.com
Facebook Page Search - THESAVVYBUSINESS
Building Business Credit System - BusinessCreditAsap.com
Facebook Page Search - Business Credit Asap